P9-DDH-998

"*Making Good* is a must-read for anyone looking to follow their passion and make money doing so. In their introspective account of modern-day trailblazers looking to 'do well by doing good,' Billy and Dev are truthful and inspiring about how to make a positive impact in a constantly changing world."

—*Jigar Shah, founder of SunEdison*

"My generation, I'm afraid, has let our dear country go into steep decline, but *Making Good* by two of our brightest young people offers solid hope for rebirth. It does that the only true and lasting way, by inspiring people at the personal level to a new way of thinking, living and working."

—*Gus Speth, former administrator of United Nations Development Program*

"This book cuts through the illusion of the quick fix and offers real solutions to help you create a life that both makes money and changes the world."

—*Sara Horowitz, president of Freelancers Union*

"Billy Parish and Dev Aujla embarked on a remarkably ambitious book. Not content to educate and mobilize on global warming and social justice, they have written a how-to book for ethical living in a corrupt economy. It is a practical guide to ensure that 'making a living' does not compromise 'having a life.' *Making Good* could change the world."

—*Elizabeth May, leader of the Green Party of Canada,*
author of Global Warming for Dummies

"This is not only the real deal—it has to be one of the most important and essential reads of today. What you can learn here will help create the positive shifts we all so desperately crave."

—*David de Rothschild, author of* The Live Earth Global Warming Survival
Handbook *and founder of Adventure Ecology*

"As individuals, as a generation, and as a species, we live at a moment of decision—the globalized problems we face implicate us all in the future of humanity. We need paradigm shifts in thinking to transform crises into opportunity. Aujla and Parish have shared a radically empowering outlook and method, as well as their own stories of navigating the challenges of inspiration and hopelessness, or making a living and making a difference. This book leaves us no excuses for not becoming the powerful agents of positive change that we dream of."

—*Severn Cullis-Suzuki, environment and culture activist and author of* Notes from Canada's Young Activist

"*Making Good* is a motivating and practical guide for the personal desire, and global urgency, to align our economics with our well-being."

—*Josh Thome, National Geographic Emerging Explorer and* 4REAL *TV series co-creator*

"*Making Good* is a fun read, full of interesting anecdotes, and useful tools. Its light tone, however, should not obscure the authors' important mission. Beneath the surface, this is a serious and timely guidebook to finding a career with meaning. It should be read by anyone who aspires to a job that will satisfy their heart without sacrificing their bank account."

—*Andrew Heintzman, author of* The New Entrepreneurs: Building a Green Economy for the Future *and president of Investeco*

MAKING GOOD

FINDING MEANING, MONEY, AND COMMUNITY IN A CHANGING WORLD

BILLY PARISH
AND
DEV AUJLA

RODALE

Mention of specific companies, organizations, or authorities in this book does not imply endorsement by the author or publisher, nor does mention of specific companies, organizations, or authorities imply that they endorse this book, its author, or the publisher.

Internet addresses and telephone numbers given in this book were accurate at the time it went to press.

© 2012 by Billy Parish and Dev Aujla

All rights reserved. No part of this publication may be reproduced or transmitted in any form or by any means, electronic or mechanical, including photocopying, recording, or any other information storage and retrieval system, without the written permission of the publisher.

Rodale books may be purchased for business or promotional use or for special sales. For information, please write to:
Special Markets Department, Rodale, Inc., 733 Third Avenue, New York, NY 10017

Printed in the United States of America
Rodale Inc. makes every effort to use acid-free ∞, recycled paper ♻.

Book design by Sara Stemen

Library of Congress Cataloging-in-Publication Data

Parish, Billy.
    Making good : finding meaning, money, and community in a changing world / Billy Parish and Dev Aujla.
        p.   cm.
    Includes bibliographical references.
    ISBN 978–1–60529–078–2   paperback
    1. Social change.   2. Community development.   3. Self-realization.
4. Self-actualization (Psychology)   I. Aujla, Dev.   II. Title.
HM831 .P375   2012
303.4—dc23   2011048001

Distributed to the trade by Macmillan

2   4   6   8   10   9   7   5   3   paperback

RODALE.

We inspire and enable people to improve their lives and the world around them.
www.rodalebooks.com

For all the people who were with us through The Wilderness

CONTENTS

INTRODUCTION

BY VAN JONES

Maybe you're like me. Maybe you've always been a little sensitive, one of those people who is moved to act when you see people suffering.

Maybe you have wondered why. Why were you seared by seeing injustices that your cousins or even close friends simply ignored? Why were you motivated to take on problems that others said were impossible to solve?

And why were you so intrigued by this book, when so many skipped right past it? Let me offer you one possible explanation: Maybe you were born for a reason.

The whole human drama—with all of its promise and peril—has been leading up to this very moment. Maybe it is not an accident that you came into this world at this time, when we need you the most.

Perhaps you are one of a special breed of people who are born to rethink old systems, uplift the downtrodden, and bring new light and new ideas into this world.

Society has many names for such people: Change makers. Social entrepreneurs. Activists. Visionaries. But the labels do little to resolve the confusion within you about what specifically you are called to do—or how you might actually do it.

It can be a struggle to discover what your particular contribution is, what unique difference you can make in the world.

This book can help you figure out how to use your talent and your calling. I am glad that you found it. In addition to its wisdom, I will give you three pointers of my own, in the hopes that you will find them useful.

The first suggestion seems too simple and obvious to mention, but it is not. This is the one step that so many people never get around to taking: *Begin.* Just take one step—any step—toward improving any situation that troubles you. If you care about kids, do something—anything—to help any kid or group of kids. Just by doing something, by beginning to act, you will separate yourself from all the people who are endlessly talking about what needs to be done, or what someone else ought to do—but who never get around to actually doing much themselves.

Number two: *Stick to it.* Ignore the haters and the doubters, even those within yourself. Just keep going. Making serious change is not a simple one-step process. We are constantly sold myths about "great people" who seemed to drive straight ahead, from victory to victory, from great achievement and contribution to great achievement and contribution.

That almost never happens in real life. In your journey, there will be great successes as well as setbacks. Each has something to teach to you.

There will be doubters. Being on that personal and social edge and feeling the pushback will enable you to learn how to make great use of everyone else's doubts, including your own. It will make you stronger, better, and carry you through so you never have to give in.

If you choose to be a change maker, most of the time it will feel like you are up against the world. That is because you are on the leading edge of a new generation. If you have a great idea (or even a little seed of one) inside you, you are trying to plant it in the asphalt to grow.

I am now on my fourth start-up enterprise, and I have never had a single idea that anyone but me thought was a good idea at first. In fact, really good ideas usually don't get a lot of agreement at first. This is why it is so important for you to take that stand even when other people think you don't have it right. To keep listening, to keep adapting, but to not abandon your vision and the approach you want to try.

When you give a speech and nobody claps, it doesn't mean that what you are saying is wrong. If you write a grant asking for $100,000 and you get $5,000, it doesn't mean you have a $5,000 idea. You may have a million-dollar idea, you just haven't learned how to express it properly.

Number three: *Take this book seriously.* Within this small tome are many of the tools you need to identify, build, and then communicate your idea as a million-dollar idea, overcoming your doubts and transforming both yourself and the world around you. You will learn the greatest skill that you need throughout your career: to be able to see problems from afar and and mobilize all your new skills to solve them quickly.

You will be able to walk into any room, any meeting, and bring a clear head and a determined heart. You are going to be able to stand out, find solutions, and make a difference. Getting out there and trying to actually make a difference creates a change in you that is just as valuable as whatever change you create in the world.

We don't know yet if we are going to be in a continued vicious downward cycle politically, economically, culturally, and spiritually—or whether this is just volatility preceding a beautiful rebirth and rebuilding. We could be entering a world of war and austerity—and all the misery that comes with that—or we could be seeing the beginnings of a positive ecological U-turn, one in which democracy is renewed by a new generation taking the stage with new information technology and cooperation tools and the economy is renewed by new models of commerce that respect people and the earth. We just don't know.

What we do know is that it is in the hands of this new generation that is shaking everything up all around the world. We know that it matters how many people go out into the streets and protest. It matters how many people decide they want a career that does good.

That's why people are so excited about the Kivas and the Kickstarters and the Solar Mosaics, the Airbnb's and the Zipcars and all of these social-purpose companies and business-savvy nonprofits. It is not going to be just about the hybrid cars—it is going to be about the hybrid models of getting things done in communities where government and private and nonprofit all start to cooperate better to get things done. We are taking some of these incredible assets our civilization has developed and redirecting them for good.

Rebuilding this economy is not just a technological challenge, it is a moral challenge. Only your generation is diverse enough, loving enough, determined enough, and connected enough to meet the true moral challenge that we face. We need to create a green economy that Dr. King would be proud of, an economy that has a place in it for everybody. You have the ability and power to do that.

Every time you add a zero to the number of people in the new generation who are adding their shoulder to the wheel of change, the level of hope and promise goes up exponentially on the planet. From 100 to 1,000, that's pretty good. Ten thousand people and you're really moving. A hundred thousand people that are concerned and mobilized can solve a lot of big problems. But you get a million people who are young enough to care and old enough to do something about it, now you hit a tipping point that can change the whole world.

That is the real promise of the book: that it will be not just a spark, but a log on the fire for a generation that is looking for real answers. As somebody who has been doing this for a while, someone twice as old as a lot of people that are involved now, it is easy to forget how a very simple question or point of confusion can hold up so much. It's like a little piece of dental floss holding up a train. Take this book as your pair of scissors. Start snipping through some of the small barriers to getting started. You have no idea where you—and your dream—will end up.

PART

THE OPPORTUNITY

CHAPTER 1

THIS MOMENT

Dev

A couple of years ago, I was at a newsstand in the airport waiting for my flight home to Toronto, chewing gum and flipping through a *Rolling Stone*. In the middle of the magazine, I came across an article about climate heroes, which featured a guy I was friends with online but—typical Facebook—had never actually met. In the picture accompanying the article, Billy Parish was standing in a cornfield in front of a school bus, which he had driven around the country on vegetable oil to raise awareness about clean energy. The words *The Dropout* were emblazoned proudly above him. *This guy,* I thought, *he's sort of like me.*

To see Billy get recognition for nontraditional work somehow made me feel like I was on the right path, made me certain the work I was doing was valid too. I had started an organization in Canada called DreamNow, which supports young people to get personally involved in fixing problems in their communities. Our tag line is "producing ideas that do good," and we have worked with people on a whole range of projects, from body image workshops to an energy-conservation campaign to turn off lights in hundreds of high school classrooms. The details of what Billy and I were doing were pretty different, but I sensed that we shared an investment in getting people personally involved in change.

I phoned my parents and told them to find the *Rolling Stone* article online. I'd been having this feeling that they were hoping my quest to do something meaningful would dead-end at law school. I wanted to show them someone like me was doing the kind of trailblazing work concerned less with convention than with results and that, at the very least, the editors at *Rolling Stone* thought it was heroic. My parents were into it, even though the thrill I felt didn't exactly transmit to them.

Two years later, I heard from Billy out of the blue. I was sitting at my desk at DreamNow, having transformed my scrappy little project into a social enterprise that had reached over 50,000 people and had raised over a million dollars for projects, as well as providing me with a good salary and the freedom to travel. When I got Billy's e-mail, I phoned back right away. We talked for about 30 minutes about the project that I had just finished through DreamNow that involved interviewing hundreds of young people and adults to figure out how to make money and change the world. I had turned up a foundation to support my research and developed the results into an e-book called *Occupation: Change the World*. Billy had read it and loved it.

In the half hour we talked, it was clear that we had remarkably similar ideas for what we wanted to focus on in the next few years. My research had shown me the importance of helping people find a way to get jobs that made an impact, and he had come to a similar place through his work on the climate change and Green Jobs movement. We both agreed that there was a huge need for someone to provide direction, to demystify the process, and to share the stories that we were both hearing every day. The people we each talked to and spent time with wanted to make a difference, but they didn't know how to get paid, how to build careers, how to raise families, and how to build lives without sacrificing all that they wanted. We had heard stories of Nobel Prize winners and of wildly successful outliers, but what about the rest of us?

I remember feeling hesitant the moment I realized the similarities between what Billy and I each wanted to do. I have always thought that there are two types of people—those who obsessively protect their ideas and those who share them, collaborate with others, and hustle so that no one can catch up. I'd always considered myself as a member of the latter group, but still, there was this lingering selfish question in my mind—after putting so much work into my e-book research, shouldn't I just do this myself? I knew we would be stronger together, but I didn't know how collaboration on a book would work or what it would look like, and I still felt like I was figuring it all out myself.

Billy

I left Yale during the fall semester of my junior year fully intending to come back. Seven years later, even though I was technically still "on leave," I arrived at my 5-year college reunion as a party crasher. But I didn't feel sheepish coming back. I was just excited to have a good time with some old friends. I was pained to discover just how miserable many of them were. Many of my classmates had defaulted to law school, some were living at home. A few people had cleared the high bar to get low-level jobs in the Obama administration, and they were deeply frustrated at how powerless they felt in such powerful positions.

I'd heard of the "quarterlife crisis," but what was going on with these people seemed like a more permanent problem. My friends had had all this crazy ambition and talent in college, this freewheeling ability to invent and imagine. But it seemed like they hadn't found anywhere to use it, and so for most of them, it was as if they had spent their life building and learning to fly a plane and, now that they were in the air, they didn't quite know where to land.

Over dinner in the big Commons cafeteria, I talked about this observation to my friend Laura, who had taken a job at a major New York publishing house. She pointed out that my story had been an exception to that rule: I'd found work that was challenging and meaningful and fun, and somehow I was also making a really good living doing it. She thought maybe I was in a position to help others, to speak to our generation, and she thought a book on the subject could connect with people.

Talking to Laura jarred something loose, and I started thinking about how I'd gotten started on my path, how the early choices I'd made ended up working out for the best. I had done a bunch of globalization and environmental activism in my first and second years of college and went into my junior year as one of four co-chairs of the Yale Student Environmental Coalition. My three other co-chairs were focused on campus sustainability initiatives, but I wanted to organize an environmental conference for college kids across the entire Northeast. We ended up having a whole weekend of workshops, large group discussions, and late-night strategy sessions. Seventy students showed up from 30 campuses. People were excited about connecting beyond their campuses, and a core group of leaders emerged. On the final day, I pushed to create a new student network to keep us connected and allow us to run campaigns together. We formed ECO-Northeast. The conference ended with much whooping, hugging, and excited departures.

Then it all started to crumble. We found it hard to recruit new leaders who hadn't bonded at the initial conference. Other existing student networks popped up, some angrily wanting to know how the student groups we worked with at a particular campus were planning on coordinating with the student campaigns they were already supporting there. One of the networks worked with a few of the students to try to stage a coup. I felt besieged, totally unsure how I fit into this new world of student movement–building.

I actually took my first semester off to try to sort out the mess I had created. I had long conversations with all the networks that worked in the region and realized that what we needed was not another splinter in an already splintered movement. We needed a coalition to bring them all together—to allow them to develop joint campaigns, to share what they learned, to build something stronger, and to do things bigger than any of them could pull off alone. While we forged closer ties in the Northeast, the idea was spreading with new clean energy alliances forming in the Southeast, the Midwest, the West Coast, and Canada.

We started hosting conference calls with leaders from some of the campus environmental groups and decided to try an experiment: a coordinated day of action called Campus Clean Energy, with a goal of getting 25 campuses to organize events urging their administrators to power their schools with clean energy. Sixty-five campuses from across the United States and Canada signed up! We were onto something. A few months later, we tried another one—Fossil Fools' Day on April 1,

2004—to target some of the Big Oil and Big Coal companies that were blocking the clean energy economy we wanted to help build. One hundred thirty campuses signed up this time!

Several years later, the Energy Action Coalition that arose from those conference calls was the largest youth organization in the world working to solve the climate crisis, funding 80 full-time staff across 25 coalition partner organizations to work with young people on smart, effective campaigns we designed together, with an annual budget of over $4 million.

The young people I worked with through the Energy Action Coalition didn't see their participation as a hobby. It was their life's work, except too many didn't know how to make that work pay the bills. After finishing school, they were floundering. The confident spirit they brought to their activism was broken, and a series of unsuccessful job interviews and unfulfilling short-term jobs ensued.

It was the same story for millions of people who wanted to solve the world's problems but couldn't find jobs. Youth unemployment in the United States hit an all-time high in the summer of 2009. Maybe we have to take things into our own hands, I thought. Maybe we can rebuild our society and economy from the bottom-up. From all the beautiful work I knew about that was emerging all over the country, all over the world—breakthrough solar technologies, urban farms, recycling initiatives—it seemed like that process was already underway. This is the story I wanted to tell—the story of the Grand Rebuilding.

Once I hit on that idea, I needed to tell someone. I Gchatted Courtney, an activist I'd been friends with for a long time, and she instantly gave me the kind of nudge that comes up when I'm on the right track.

BILLY: i think my next big project is going to be writing a book.
COURTNEY: wow! on what?

        is it an erotic adventure novel?
BILLY: on how to make a living while saving the world . . . sort of a
    primer for people who want to be part of building the green
    economy. with some good sex stories woven in.
COURTNEY: do you know dev aujla?

I'd heard of him. He was a kind of mystical figure in the youth-organizing world in Canada. He was part of the main student environmental group I worked with there, the Sierra Youth Coalition, but he had also started a fashion company, ran his own nonprofit, and now, apparently, did green jobs stuff too. I Googled him and found an e-book he'd recently published on making money and changing the world. I felt an involuntary twinge of envy. He'd written everything that *wasn't* in the outline I had sketched for the book, all the practical nuts-and-bolts tools for personal involvement, and it was all essential stuff I wanted my readers to have.

The more I thought about it, the more I wondered if we might be able to team up. His e-book was the perfect companion for the book I wanted to write. I had an analysis about what was wrong with the major systems in our society—from energy to food to education—and how we should fix them. He wrote about the personal obstacles that so many young people face and gave really good practical advice about where to start. I had helped design a campaign to create 5 million green jobs through a Clean Energy Corps, part of which was passed into law, and he had been helping hundreds of young people launch themselves into careers with meaning.

With a little wave of relief that I might not have to take on such a massive project all by myself, I sent Dev an e-mail. A few hours later I got his call.

Dev

I met Billy for the first time at Penn Station. For the past year, I had been getting DreamNow going in the States, trying to build my network and living part-time in New York, and it was starting to feel like home. I remember Billy had wanted to meet in DC, where he had to head for an Energy Action meeting, but I was already a little nervous to meet him and thought it best to meet in a city I felt comfortable in, where I had a place to stay. So there I was, waiting on the corner, still not feeling 100 percent comfortable.

Billy came out of the train station carrying the kind of blue backpack I used to have in high school, and seeing his friendly familiarity put me instantly at ease. We said our hellos and started walking uptown. Somehow our conversation began with our grandparents' stories. I told him the cowboy stories of my mother's grandfather, who immigrated in the early 1900s from India to Canada to work on farms in Alberta and trade pigs for land. I told him about where my ambition came from— the stories from my paternal grandfather, who left his young family to come over from India illegally at the age of 23. He was caught by immigration officials and had to spend 16 years apart from his new family before finally being able to bring his then-16-year-old daughter and wife back to Canada.

My family had instilled in me the values that set me on my path, and I found out Billy felt the same way. I really wanted to work with him, but I had never even spent any time with him, and trusting someone with your identity and your ideas seemed like a big commitment.

We continued our conversation as we cut through Central Park, walking along the edge of the paved running and cycling path. As runners rushed by us, Billy asked me, "So Dev, what's your spirit animal?"

Oh my god, I thought. *This is getting really hippie, really fast.*

Billy went on to tell me these emotional stories about why his spirit animal was the firefly, how at turning points in his life—his daughter's birth, the founding of the Energy Action Coalition, in India when he realized he needed to go back to the States and dedicate himself to climate change work—fireflies were always present. His stories were amazing, but in that moment, I felt unspiritual by comparison and oddly desperate for a spirit animal. Fireflies, emotional turning points, it was all so intense. We had gotten off the running path and were walking by the turtle pond. "A turtle," I said, but I immediately felt like he knew I was making it up. So I said, "Well, I've always wanted to be a fish."

He laughed. It was okay that he and I were different. Happily, it seemed like a good thing.

Billy

At lunch, I ordered us the nova and sturgeon plate with fresh bagels and all the fixings. It was what my dad and I used to get, usually on Sunday afternoons, on our way home from my soccer, baseball, or basketball game, depending on the season. Naturally, the conversation steered toward our families. My parents divorced when I was 5, I told Dev, but lived near one another and talked every day. When we were kids, my older sister Maya and I spent a weekday and weekend night with my dad and the other five nights with our mom. Our parents didn't believe in spanking—I don't even remember any yelling—but somehow instilled a strong sense of right and wrong in us through their own example and the occasional intense stare.

Dev told me about the weekly family meetings he grew up with, where they would talk about virtues they appreciated—honesty, courage, and fairness—and what they meant to live out in practice. His parents had been inspired by a book called *The Virtues Project*, which had spurred a movement in British Columbia in the early 1990s. He recalled kicking his younger brother Aaron under the table as kind of a secret rebellion against virtue.

Even though our families had come from such different places, the values that we had been given had set us on almost parallel paths. We had built organizations, done race and class work through the environmental movement, debated whether to drop out of the university because of our excitement to get to work, and somehow figured out how to get paid for what we loved. And now we both had this long-term emphasis on devoting ourselves to work that addressed the global problems we were raised to feel responsible for solving.

But my willingness to go whole hog had changed in the past few years. In 2006, my life consisted of 100-hour workweeks, being on the road half the time, staying up nights following up with coalition partners, all the while getting my beauty sleep on floors and couches. Not exactly a calm lifestyle. One weekend that spring, Energy Action Coalition held a strategy meeting in New York City with our coalition partners. Black Mesa Water Coalition, a Navajo and Hopi organization that was working to protect the tribes' groundwater and transition their coal-based practices, sent its field director, Wahleah Johns. The woman had presence. She didn't speak much, but every time she did, you could hear a pin drop, and her words shaped the course of the group conversation, connected dots to help us figure out how our campus campaigns could help communities fighting coal mines and coal plants. I was smitten.

Wahleah and I married in 2007, and in 2008, we had our first daughter, Tohaana. Making money leaped up my life priority list. Beyond the diapers and clothes, I wanted to provide a house she could grow up in, to send her to the best schools, to save for her like my parents had saved for me. Time also became more precious. I needed to restructure my life so that I could be there for them. It was hard leaving Wahleah alone with the baby, so I raised the bar for what I would travel for. That was something else I wanted to add to our project—ideas about how to make the fabled work/life balance a reality.

Dev

At the end of the day, sitting over a Beastmaster pizza and some beer at Roberta's in Brooklyn, we made a decision to write this book together, to tell our own stories and share the stories of all the people we had met who had figured out how to build a meaningful career. Though we barely knew each other, it felt like we were ready to get started. Perhaps the reason I felt so comfortable with him was because of something neither of us knew at the time, that both of our paths that had led us to our new mission had actually started less than 200 miles apart, 10 years earlier, on the other side of the world, the Tibetan Plateau.

Billy

It was the summer after my sophomore year, and I had come to

India through a grant from Yale to support an independent research project on an innovative community forestry program that had recently been developed there.

Shortly after my arrival, I wanted to pull off a round-trip hike to the Gaumukh glacier, the source of the Ganges River that rests at the far end of a massive ice sheet deep in the Himalayas. My guide, Anand, was a young guy from the basecamp town of Gangotri with intense brown eyes that seemed to take in more than what was visible. Anand told me he had never done the round-trip 26 miles (including an elevation change of 10,000 feet to 15,000 feet) in 1 day; the trips he led were usually 3 to 4 days. As I was 21 and ready for adventure, this only egged me on.

Crossing a bridge just outside of town, I saw powerful, dark rapids slicing through a valley in the mist. As we walked into the valley, steep cliffs on either side, the river dwindled. A few hours in, we passed a tall man walking slowly up the path, barefoot in an orange robe, his long hair pulled into a bun. Anand told me that thousands of Sadhus, holy people, made the trek every year to what many considered the holiest place in India.

The Ganges, or, as Indians call it, "Gung-Ga," is worshipped as the female goddess Ganga and has been at the center of Indian spiritual, political, and economic history. For thousands of years, people have come to its banks to purify themselves in water we now understand to have powerful bacteria-killing and unusual oxygen-retaining properties. There are actually six major tributaries to the Ganges, all stemming from the glaciers of the Tibetan Plateau, but the Gaumukh is considered the headstream. This enormous river, whose basin covers nearly 400,000 square miles (a little larger than the country of Egypt), accommodates some 450 million people who come to drink, eat, farm, clean, and bathe themselves. As we approached the Gaumukh—literally "cow's mouth" in Hindi—we saw a large, white plastic tent with a satellite dish on top and a man sitting on the boulders by the river's edge. He was part of a scientific project studying glacial melt around the world. He pointed to the spot about a half mile in the direction from which we'd come, a distance the glacier had covered only 25 years earlier, and then he moved his finger to show us the farthest the glacier had reached the year before, about 100 feet down river. Now, it was at our backs. As soon as 2030, the scientist said, it could be gone.

The Western-driven industrialization that had delivered enormous benefit to people everywhere had also filled the skies with pollution so thick it was heating up the entire planet. The United States alone, with 4 percent of the world's population, contributed 25 percent of the world's carbon pollution—20 times more per person than the average Indian. As someone raised with a deep sense of right and wrong, I felt directly implicated. Recognizing the scale of the problem made me feel responsible for its solution.

We hiked up the side of the glacier, across the grayish frozen river, and up a small mountain on the far side. Anand had warned me about climbing too fast, but my head was racing and caution wasn't a concern. As I looked across the expanse of the doomed glacier and the huge valley it used to fill, I thought about all the aspects of Indian life that revolved around this place that would simply cave in. My legs started to shake, and my eyes poured out tears. I collapsed onto the ground. Anand helped me up and told me we had to get to a lower elevation to recover.

In some ways, I'm still recovering.

The following semester, I ended up dropping out of college. I was pissed off. It was almost too unfair and stupid to believe, but here it was, happening before our very eyes. Scientists were frantically sounding the alarm bells, but almost nobody seemed to be doing anything about it. Just the opposite! Only a year earlier, hopes of passing the already watered-down Kyoto Protocol were rejected as too strong, and Big Coal and Big Oil companies continued to dominate energy policy. It was time to get involved.

Dev

I had approached this guy named Peter Dalgish after he spoke at a conference at my high school. I was the keen kid who rushed the speaker after the talk wanting to know more. After all of the people faded out of the room, I was still hanging around trying to get any last information about his organization, Street Kids International. At the time, he was working with the International Labor Organization, helping to lead and run its programs for kids in Kathmandu. "You should come and visit me in Nepal," he told me. "These kids need you." It was one of those comments that he must have thrown out to hundreds of people, but when he said it, I took it to heart. I couldn't think of anything I wanted to do more.

Two years and many e-mails later, I got on a plane with my brother, Aaron, who was in grade 12, and headed to Kathmandu.

I'd never been able to imagine Kathmandu beyond its reference in a John Lennon song and childhood rhymes, but when I landed in that valley in the Himalayas, it became an unworldly reality—noise, chaos, and the buzz of people everywhere.

Aaron and I quickly learned that we were going to be staying and working at a school where children came to live from rural and impoverished areas, sometimes 7 days from the nearest

road. Their parents were often absent, sometimes political pris-
oners, always extremely poor. The children who came to live at
the school were getting another chance.

During our stay, I became friends with a boy named Urgen
Tenzig. He was 12 years old but looked like a boy of 7 or 8
because of malnourishment. He had come to the school from
the foot hills of the Himalayas, and because of neglect, he had
not seen his parents for over 2 years. One of the days I was there
was his birthday, and he was totally lit up. What made this day
even more special was the fact that earlier that morning,
Urgen's mother had called the school's office with a message for
him—his parents would pick him up that night at 6 p.m. They
would be reunited for his birthday.

Urgen wanted to give a gift to his parents, as it had been so
long since he last saw them. We went out through Boudha, the
Buddhist district, looking for the perfect gift. We found it—a
sugar-covered cake donut on which Urgen spent 35 rupees
(about the equivalent of 70 cents). This was a lot of money for a
boy who had none, almost everything he had.

Soon enough, we were back at the school and I was sitting
with Urgen during his study hour. His cake was on the desk in
a little black plastic bag, and his eyes were batting between his
watch and me and his watch again. There was no hope to get
him to study . . . it was 6, then it was 6:30, and then it was 7 . . .

By bedtime, it was clear that Urgen's parents weren't going to
come. I had the distinct sense that Urgen's entire ability to experience hope and joy was riding on this moment. All Urgen wanted
for his birthday was to hug his parents. And instead, he waited
and waited, with only me, a relative stranger, to console him.

I told him, "Urgen, something probably came up. I'm sure

your parents will be here tomorrow, and you will get to spend the whole day with them."

Urgen looked at me sadly, and in that moment, I realized all those things that were comfortable certainties in my life, the support of my family, my home in Canada, all made it impossible for me to understand what was going on in his. Urgen looked back up at me, and he said, "It doesn't matter, Dev. It doesn't matter because tomorrow isn't my birthday."

My brother and I took Urgen and several of his friends up to our room, set out the cake donut, turned up the music, and threw him a birthday party. Smiles filled the room, and I felt great that I'd been able to lighten the mood.

Still, I felt it wasn't enough. I'd only made a difference in this localized way, for this one moment. No good time could really make up for the fact that Urgen's parents weren't around. But wasn't I in an excellent position to do this on a larger scale, for more people, with a lasting impact? I felt I had to act—if I could just show up and make a small difference, imagine what I could do if I decided to really commit myself to improving people's lives.

I came back to the university and I stepped into that understanding. I began to help others start community projects with the vision that, one project at a time, I could help transform communities and actually make an impact.

Chances are, at some point in your life, you decided that you needed to spend your time on making this world right. Maybe it was a gradual feeling, or maybe it was a defining moment in the same way that Dev felt on Urgen's birthday, in the way Billy felt looking out at the Gaumukh glacier. You are not alone.

It often starts with an unformed emotional response to something you see or read about, a feeling of anger or sadness that you just can't shake. Bending your mind around the prevalence of genocide in our world, of rape, of hunger, of pestilential sickness, of the 27 million people in slavery today—that isn't easy. We're occasionally able to experience these moments where we connect and actually understand the pain of others, humans as well as other fellow living things, in a way that has the power to change us forever.

In 1990, a climate scientist named Paul Crutzen gave the geological period of time that we currently all live in a name that stuck: the Anthropocene. Human civilization has defined the geological features of the age. We have grown so big so quickly, we've damaged the basic life-supporting systems on the planet. Freshwater grows scarce, topsoils deplete, toxic chemicals flood every corner, and the atmosphere thickens with carbon pollution from fossil fuels. Between sprawling development, deforestation, and unsustainable levels of consumption, we have triggered a mass extinction, with some 30,000 species vanishing from the planet forever every year.[1] We've made a mess of our only home, and the people who are least responsible for the damage are the hardest hit.

How we respond is different for each of us, but there's a common feeling that defines the experience: empathy. Empathy is different from sympathy or pity, feelings that preserve an uninvolved distance. Empathy connects us to the realities of others, makes us feel their emotions and experiences as we feel

[1] International Union for Conservation of Nature (IUCN) 2011. *Red List of Threatened Species.* www.iucnredlist.org

our own, and it's what makes us as humans feel that desire to do something, to not just passively stand by when there is injustice, or join in when there is hope. We are actually hardwired to feel this way, to feel compassion and togetherness when someone else is in trouble, to feel implicated in their well-being.

All across the world, people are waking up to this feeling. It's almost as if a global alarm has gone off, calling us collectively into action in a way that feels brand new. And with the added urgency we all feel to find paying work, many people are driving positive change through business, converting possibility into reality, and discovering lives that are more fun, more prosperous, and more meaningful. The people channeling these feelings into lifelong careers are the architects of our future. We've come to think of them as Rebuilders.

These are people like Marcos Bittencourt, who employs hundreds of people across Brazil to collect plastic bottles and make affordable fishing nets and other products for small farmers. People like Sarah Scarborough, whose travels took her from organic farms in Australia to the founding of Partners Tea Company in Nashville, which donates 1 percent of sales to empower women through education. Fashion designers like Natalia Allen, who won Parsons' Designer of the Year award for her work with sustainable fabrics and innovative design. These people are spread across the professional spectrum, from presidents to assistants, but all channeling that same commitment to find meaning, money, and community while making a better world.

This movement of Rebuilders is riding a wave of three tectonic shifts in the way our world operates.

One of the most significant, visible changes in our world is that for the first time in history, across divisions of race and class, country and religion, we are beginning to see ourselves as one family. After the attacks of 9/11, the sentiment from remote villages in Africa to subdivisions in Arkansas was *We Are All New Yorkers*. When the people of Tunisia rose up against an oppressive dictator in 2011, they started a domino effect that sparked a new courage across the Arab world to demand governments accountable to the people. Our innate empathy now extends to the whole planet.

Bestselling author and economist Jeremy Rifkin lays out in *The Empathic Civilization* a question that speaks to this rise of a global empathy. He asks, "If we have gone from empathy in blood ties, to empathy in religious associational ties, to empathy based on national identification, is it really a big stretch to imagine the new technologies allowing us to connect our empathy writ large to the human race in a single biosphere?" It's not a stretch, and we can do more than imagine it. Millions of people all over the world already are tapping into a sense of empathy, connecting over common values centered on fairness, freedom, and care of the planet.

Another monumental change in the way we live today is that the Internet has given us new tools to easily, instantaneously collaborate, innovate, and share information across borders. Wikipedia democratizes the public record, hundreds of thousands of sites revolve on the momentum of user-generated reviews, advice, and feedback, and social networking gives us the impression of intimacy across great distances. Linux has pioneered methods of open-source software development and has become one of the most popular operating systems in the world. Twitter has quite literally redefined our conception of how news breaks and who breaks it. Each of us has an arsenal of information-gathering and communication tools more sophisticated than the entire US government had only 20 years ago. There's opportunity to contribute and collaborate in ways large and small, with varying levels of expertise, in every field, from wherever you are.

The third change is that a wave of smarter and greener technology is comprehensively reinventing the way we live. New industrial processes sustainably manufacture goods at a fraction of the cost of current methods. Clean-tech is making breakthroughs in everything from batteries that power electric cars, to thin-film solar collectors that can cover the surface of any building, to algae-based fuels that could replace jet fuel. Advances like permaculture and drip irrigation have the potential to sustainably and dramatically increase crop yields and lift millions of families out of poverty. We're now limited more by what we can dream up than what's technically possible.

The rise of a global empathy, the Internet as a platform for global collaboration, and breakthrough technologies—these three trends have fused into a formula that doesn't just give people the ambition, it gives them tools and the power to change the world for the better. The result is what may yet be the largest movement in the history of civilization.

In some ways, what's most remarkable about this movement is that it's both global and thoroughly intergenerational. From Tinebeb Yohannes, a young girl in Ethiopia who organized a march of more than 15,000 people in the streets of Addis Ababa for 350.org's first international day of action on climate change, to Ray Anderson, who woke up to the perils of climate change and toxic pollution in his early sixties, and as the CEO of Interface, the largest carpet company in the world, became a leading voice for sustainable business. No generation ever remakes the world on its own.

As has been true for most major social change movements throughout history, young people are leading the way. We're burning with the same energy our parents' generation was, but young people today are doing things differently. While outrage was once a foundational piece of political change, it doesn't have nearly the same unifying call as it did back then. That doesn't make us less engaged; it just means that we're meeting the world's needs in a different, more networked way and with a changing set of tools. Rather than effecting change through confrontation, we are uniting in huge numbers through social networking. Instead of polarizing people who don't agree with us, we are seducing them with business models that are more creative, sustainable, and profitable. We don't want our involvement in change to be a phase of youth. We want to make it a life, a job.

But we are the children of what was a revolutionary (and remarkably effective) generation in its own right. The Boomers fought for and won civil rights, an end to the war in Vietnam, the Environmental Protection Act, and the Charter of Rights and Freedoms. Our parents and grandparents are beginning to calculate the impacts of a lifetime of unsustainable consumption and are using their still considerable institutional and financial power to finish what they started. Others are beginning their "encore careers" to build a safer, more stable world for their kids and grandkids to enjoy.

Often social change is stymied by a generational culture clash—young people rebelling against the values, culture, and structures of our parents. But that's not really going on today.

In our experience, young change makers relate to and respect the work their parents' generation did. We like the music and the style, the speeches still inspire us. More than anything, we want our elders as partners in the change process.

We're still figuring out how to make generational collaboration work, and sometimes it feels clumsy, but when generations work together and assets and skill sets combine, we get revolutionary companies. Sungevity, with a staff of nearly 350 people in its Oakland, California, headquarters that is growing almost daily, has brought the entire process of selling and financing home solar installations online, using satellite mapping to assess rooftops for solar potential and software to design custom systems. Its team combines grayhairs, people who bring deep finance expertise, with young and vibrant sales, design, and social media groups.

Muhammad Yunus, now in his seventies, started the Grameen bank to bring microfinance to Bangladesh but has recruited energetic innovators of all ages to launch a family of companies spanning telecommunications, energy, microfinance, healthcare, agriculture, and textile sectors that employ thousands and empower millions of people to pull themselves out of poverty through sustainable business. Grameenphone is the largest tax-paying company in Bangladesh, with over 25 million subscribers and 400,000 "telephone ladies" who sell telephone services, a call at a time, to those without phones of their own.[2]

Globally, more venture capital dollars are being directed

---

[2] Yunus, Muhammad, and Karl Weber. *Creating a World without Poverty: Social Business and the Future of Capitalism*. New York: PublicAffairs, 2007.

toward clean energy systems than fossil fuels.[3] Organics are the fastest-growing segment of the US food market.[4] Fifty-nine percent of all companies across industries increased their investments in sustainability in 2010, which is up from just 25 percent in 2009.[5] Networks like the Business Alliance for Local Living Economies (BALLE) represent over 22,000 businesses across the United States and Canada that are committed to doing good and doing well. Seventy percent of graduates across North America are now looking for jobs with companies that have a good reputation in corporate social responsibility.[6] Governments, corporations, and consumers have all responded, shifting the economic playing field and opening up enormous new markets for sustainable products and services of all kinds.

The opportunity we have today is to build a new foundation by recreating the major systems that organize our world. A senior VP for a large grocery chain in his late fifties who we interviewed essentialized this beautifully: "My generation made its money tearing the world apart and your generation is going to make its money putting it back together."

To be involved, you don't have to be a 5-year planner, a type-A person, or an extrovert. This opportunity is also not just for entrepreneurs and Fortune 500 companies. There are equally important roles to play (and benefits to claim) for so-called "intrapreneurs," individuals who make change from the inside

---

[3] United Nations Environment Program, SEFI, and New Energy Finance. *Global Trends in Sustainable Energy Investment*. Rep. New York: 2009.

[4] "ERS/USDA Data— Organic Production." *USDA Economic Research Service*. United States Department of Agriculture, 14 Sept. 2010.

[5] Boston Consulting Group, and MIT Sloan Management. *Sustainability: The 'Embracers' Seize Advantage*. Rep. Boston: MIT Sloan Managment Review, 2011.

[6] Robinson, Oliver. "Planning for a Fairer Future." *The Guardian* [London] 14 July 2006.

of existing companies and organizations. There is opportunity enough for all of us.

"The difference between what we do and what we are capable of doing would suffice to solve most of the world's problems."

—MAHATMA GANDHI

According to the International Labor Organization, as of 2010, 211 million people around the world were officially out of work. When we factor in the underemployed and those of us who have given up looking for a job, the number climbs much higher. And if there isn't a radical shift in the direction of our economy, there will be no relief: According to some estimates, in the next 10 years, only 300 million new jobs will appear to greet the billion young people entering the workforce.[7]

In this desperate landscape, millions of us are resigning ourselves to work that hurts us, hurts others, and damages the planet. We're wasting our greatest assets. We have a deep, dim sense that there's something else we're meant for, but we don't know exactly where the opportunities are or how to access them.

That's what this book is about. Even though we care and we're intellectually invested in efforts to rebuild our world, trying to figure out how to personally participate in the movement in progress, given the need and complications in our personal lives, can be a challenge. How do we translate the desire

[7] "Investment Strategies for Youth." *Youth Employment and Entrepreneurship.* ImagineNations, 2010.

to do something good into a rich and sustaining life path that effects real change?

Given the complicated networks of expectations, habits, and desires, this isn't easy for any of us. The road to designing one's work life is jammed with riddles and paradoxes. We want to make money, to have the things that our televisions promise will deliver happiness with a money-back guarantee, but we don't want to sell out. We want to feel resilient through recessions and upswings, we want financial security in the face of record personal debt, to consume and indulge according to our moods in a time when we are reaching peak levels of resource availability. We want stability, but we also want freedom. We want to make the people we love proud. We want to stand against trends that bother us philosophically, but we don't want to check out of the culture.

We feel like we have no time. We're afraid to take risks. We work more hours for less pay than North Americans did a generation ago.[8] We have more stuff, more luxury, and more ways to be entertained; yet, we are less happy.

We wanted to write a book not only to relate our personal experiences and the global systemic struggles that challenge us as a generation, but also to help anyone of any age understand how to take advantage of the enormous new opportunities to change the world. We will need to rethink, redesign, and rebuild nearly everything, from the way we construct buildings to the way we get our food into our homes. That process is underway, but it is far from complete. We must prepare for it in the simple

[8] Luce, Edward. "Crisis of middle-class america." *Financial Times* 30 July 2010.

daily rituals and in the invisible coalitions that stretch across our towns, across our country, and across the planet.

But first, a caution. This book is not a quick fix. Today there is a cultural promise that is echoed everywhere: *Anything is possible if you believe (or if you buy)*. The promise comes packaged in trendy books or aspirational shows on TV. It's the American dream refreshed for today's audience.

But there are cracks in this cultural promise. Real change—for your life and for the world—doesn't happen in the form of a 20-minute episode (or in the 10 minutes of commercials on most cable shows). A generation swept up into a movement built on *Hope* ran headlong into the overwhelming complexity of making *Change*. How can we build a clean-tech company that competes with Big Oil's billions in annual subsidies by "just doing it"? How can you start a business while trying to manage $60,000 or $100,000 in student loans?

To help you get beyond doubt, we share the lessons we've learned that help people find the confidence to begin. These lessons are distilled from our interviews with hundreds of people we've lived and worked with over the past 10 years. They range from major players on the international scene to organic farmers at the local market. They are the stories that locate a sweet spot between altruism and selfishness, between the individual and the collective.

We also share our own experiences. How Billy has been able to raise over $12 million, invest in promising clean-tech companies, and launch his own solar company. How Dev started his own nonprofit in Canada, developed a sustainable revenue stream, and raised over $3 million for youth-led projects in Canada. How Billy launched Solar Mosaic from the home he bought in Flagstaff, while Dev rented apartments in both New York and Toronto in order to pursue an opportunity with a visionary social change—focused company. But even more important, we share the lessons we've each used to build powerful friendships and strong support networks, to develop our skills, and to live out our values, all while finding time to have fun with friends and family.

We introduce practical strategies, exercises, and resources designed to help you recognize, organize, and fully exploit your inherent potential to do great things. Each chapter includes a unique daily practice that we've adapted from Billy's experience at the Rockwood Leadership Institute's Leading from the Inside Out yearlong training, led by Robert Gass. The Rockwood Leadership Institute is the premier progressive leadership training institute in the United States, offering yearlong intensives, fellowships, and 3- to 5-day trainings. Every year, 24 of the country's most influential social change leaders are invited to participate in the yearlong intensive training.

Rockwood's programs are about "leadership from the inside out," based on a belief that transformation starts from within. The goal is to take overworked (or already-burned-out) individuals and provide them with a set of tools, strategies, and practices that allow them to be more effective with less effort and to sustain work over many years. We are sharing Gass's daily practices for the first time, and we hope you'll find them to be powerful and grounding lessons to help you on your own path.

The practices contain action steps that you can just follow as you read, but for a deeper experience, you can also sign up at makinggood.org to get the daily practices e-mailed to you each morning. Each practice has steps that can be worked on over a period of 3 to 4 weeks to begin to really incorporate the practice into your daily habits.

This book can help you find the satisfaction in designing your external life so that it reflects your internal principles. And finding that balance isn't just about happiness. At this moment, it's about meeting your own potential to help rebuild a world in desperate need.

DAILY PRACTICE #1: OUR CHOICE

"I have come to the frightening conclusion that I am the decisive element. It is my personal approach that creates the climate. It is my daily mood that makes the weather. I possess tremendous power to make life miserable or joyous. I can be a tool of torture or an instrument of inspiration. I can humiliate or humor, hurt or heal. In all situations, it is my response that decides whether a crisis is escalated or de-escalated, and a person is humanized or de-humanized. If we treat people as they are, we make them worse. If we treat people as they ought to be, we help them become what they are capable of becoming."
—JOHANN WOLFGANG VON GOETHE

STEP 1: SEE YOURSELF

Let's start with a question about your own life. Ask yourself: *"When and where am I feeling like I don't have any choice?"*

This feeling is often expressed as "I have to . . ." or "I can't . . ." or some variation thereof.

I have to finish this report.

I can't get through my whole inbox.

I've got to return this call.

I can't organize my files.

I can't get to the gym today.

I can't focus.

My boss/partner told me I have to be more efficient.

I have to stay in touch with my contacts.

I can't stick to a budget.

I don't have time to devote to others.

I can't learn all I need to know to start this project.

I can't find balance in my life.

Reflect right now for a few minutes and make your own list. Are there certain situations where this happens more? Do you tend to relate to certain people with more of a sense of obligation? Are there some persistent "have to's" in your life where you regularly experience a perceived lack of choice?

STEP 2: NOTICE OTHERS

Once you become aware of your own "have to's," you will probably start to notice a lot of this dead-end behavior in your

environment. You may notice it in people who have every reason to feel victimized by the circumstances of their birth,
race, and social identity. You may find it in people with little
"real" power or wealth. If you're alert, you will also find it in
people with considerable external power and privilege.

But remember, almost all communication is nonverbal.
Many of the signs of victimhood will be in someone's tone,
whether it's whiny, bitter, anxious, discouraged, frustrated, or
depressed. You can also sometimes detect it in body postures,
such as slumped shoulders and crossed arms. Really listen to
the conversations around your life, your circles of colleagues
and friends. Notice when the groups of people or even entire
communities in your life submit to "I have to" and "I can't."

To what degree do people support each others' victimization? Do you or people you know get stuck in the loop of "ain't
it awful" affirmations?

PERSON 1: "I can't find a good-paying job anywhere—no one is
hiring."
PERSON 2: "Yeah, ain't it awful?"

Or are there norms of engaging and inspiring each other
to test the limits of what's possible? To what extent can we push
conversations infused with a dead-end energy to open up to the
broad spectrum of all that's possible?

At a societal level, there is real victimization, and many in
this world are indeed oppressed. We see psychological and
physical suffering caused by injustice everywhere. There is
inadequate access to basics of human survival, and people are

32

dying as a result of greed-driven structures and systems. Many people have every good reason to feel victimized.

But ultimately, we choose how to feel about our circumstances and also how to respond to them. Each moment, that choice is renewed. Each day, we have the power to choose how we show up to each individual situation—each experience is a new chance, no matter what happened yesterday. One hundred percent responsibility invites us to continually examine and claim our choices, to find dignity and power even when our gut tells us there is none. Consider the words of Austrian psychiatrist and concentration camp survivor Viktor Frankl: "I saw too many people give away their last morsel of food, their last sip of water to others in need to know that no one can take away the last of our human freedoms—the freedom to choose our own way, in whatever the circumstances."

Begin the practice of noticing how the people you interact with show up. Is the world out of their control or do they have choice? Decide for yourself what person you are choosing to be within each distinct interaction.

STEP 3: RECOGNIZE YOUR CHOICES

Next time you feel there isn't any option, try these four strategies to shift from feeling like you don't have any choice to finding yourself in control.

1. Ask questions. What are my obvious options? What choices do I have that I'm not recognizing? What are some minor ways I might approach things differently? And some larger ways? How can I rearrange my external approach? And my internal approach?

2. Move from past to future. Shift your thinking from fixation on the past (wishing for a different history or regretting choices, neither of which we can do anything to change) to the present and future (what I can do right now and what do I want going forward).

3. Work with "if" phrases. If I were taking complete responsibility, I would _____. If I fully owned my power, I would_____.

4. Change your physical state. Sometimes just getting out of your chair and going for a short walk can give you perspective and help you recognize all the choices you have. Try deepening your breathing, tensing and relaxing your muscles, putting on some music and dancing, working out, practicing yoga, or doing whatever you like to do to get physical.

This perspective is foundational to the work of rebuilding. We need to genuinely believe that things can change, that what once seemed impossible is now within reach. Arriving at that perspective is largely a matter of seeking and claiming our options, from the tiniest task-related choice, to the sweeping global choices we make as a culture. Do we really have to trade our time for money for something we don't believe? Do we have to settle for being unhappy at work just because we have the pressure of bills to pay?

We can seek that sense of agency on a global scale as well. Do we have to let a billion people go hungry every day when we have more than enough food to feed them all? Do we have to destroy communities and the planet by tapping and burning fossil fuels when the sun provides more energy in an hour than all the coal mines and oil wells do in a year?

Change starts with the simple belief in progress. And to participate in progress, we have to take hold of the millions of choices that come together to create the arrow of change. The world needs your best self. You need your best self right now. Let's get started.

CHAPTER 2

STEPPING UP

"There is a vitality, a life force, an energy, a quickening, that is translated through you into action. And because there is only one of you in all time, this expression is unique. If you block it, it will never exist through any other medium and will be lost. The world will not have it. It is not your business to determine how good it is, nor how it compares to other expressions. It is simply your business to keep the channel open."
— MARTHA GRAHAM

Sometimes it can seem like really successful people developed their careers while the rest of us were still doing our homework. In reality, career success is an evolutionary process. To demystify that process, we sent an e-mail to some established Rebuilder friends with a simple form, asking them to describe for us what they do for a living and how they came into their work. When we read through their responses, we found that not only was their path to success circuitous, but—perhaps more important—the notion of a simple, definable occupation doesn't apply to people finding the work that is making good in this changing world.

Looking through the forms we got back, we realized how hard it is to come up with job titles that capture the sequence of schooling, internships, jobs, and other experiments and activities of even one of the hundreds of individuals we spoke to. Teacher, financier, or career planner can't do justice to the constantly evolving career paths so many people are taking today.

Take our friend Jen. For the past 4 years, she's been establishing herself as a feminist oral historian, working for a foundation recording the stories of women who played a major role in Canada's history. One night, back at her family's house for dinner at home in Vancouver, she was given a business card by her mother, who told her, "Here, this person has an interesting job title." The card read *Leslie Bancroft, Vice President for Shareholder Communications*. Jen looked at the card in confusion. What did this have to do with her? "Don't contact her, but take a look," her mother said, noticing her daughter's expression. "Maybe it's something you'd want to do?"

This is the struggle of one generation trying to understand another. A mother wonders how it can be possible for her daughter to achieve stability with a job title she made up herself. Dev gets the same reaction from his family. Every Christmas he enjoys hearing his father explain to relatives and friends what he is doing. It changes every year. One year, his father put him at the helm of a think tank; the next, he was anointed a lobbyist.

We all struggle with the cultural promises guaranteeing stability, jobs that lead to affluent lives, or positions of power. The stories in our culture make it easy to envision what the future looks like when following a well-trodden path. One can see the kids, the house with the pool in the backyard, the drive to work, and the consistency and stability that come as a result of the long hours and slow climb up a company or law firm's internal staircase. You will be *all set*.

It has become something of a joke with a number of our high-achieving friends that whenever they go home to speak with their parents, they will be asked: *"Have you given any thought to law school?"* No matter how successful they are, the classic career narrative is something our parents' generation understands well.

But the promise is a fantasy. In the housing bubble, in the collapse of corporations amid scandal, in the financial meltdown, in the trillions of dollars vanished, and in the millions of workers in mainstream professions who lost their "stable" jobs. Construction workers got it worst, but dozens of other professions we considered stable—finance, real estate, medicine, and marketing—got a dramatic reality check in the last recession, just as "normal jobs" have time and time again throughout history. Each time, what we thought and knew to be the safe bets for careers were taken away from us. The story we tell ourselves gives us such an impermeable sense of confidence that even when that story is revealed as a myth, our friends can still count on having to explain why law school isn't for them.

Stepping into a life that makes good is hard in part because we don't have the cultural narrative that provides us with that same impermeable confidence that we are going to have a stable, meaningful career. Without that story, life can feel like a perpetual battle, defending our choices, worrying about our futures, and facing frustration when our explanations of what our lives will look like doesn't compress easily onto the face of a business card.

But if we want to be on the leading edge, if we want to take advantage of the real opportunities that are presenting themselves today, we are going to have to find our confidence not in the mainstream cultural narratives, but in the stories we live out ourselves. Staring down doubt is a skill, a practice, and if it's any comfort, virtually all of the people we interviewed for the book identified doubt as a major obstacle to building a career of meaning. These feelings are natural—risk is not something we have been trained for.

This chapter is about understanding a life path that many of us are choosing to walk. It's a path that doesn't always impart a consistent job title, where meaning can become a method to achieve financial stability, where our instinctive emotional response to the injustices in our world lays the foundation for a long-term career. We build this path ourselves, our purpose evolving as we go, and we are carried through by our consistent commitment to doing good.

Figuring out what to do with your life isn't just about self-examination—it's about examination of the world you live in. Theologian Frederick Buechner puts it this way: "Your vocation is where your greatest passion meets the world's greatest need." It takes a conscious act of imagining beyond what you see, connecting what you read and what you understand about the world to the actual life you lead.

Building the path ourselves means that we need to find strength and confidence in new ways. We need to equip ourselves with different sets of tools. In analyzing the stories of successful Rebuilders, we've identified four stages their paths share in common. Anticipating these stages can help you find the confidence to pursue this new path and navigate through a life of meaning and success.

STAGE 1: THE WILDERNESS

We all enter The Wilderness at different times in our lives and for different reasons. For the more privileged among us, we may not really see or feel the disharmony, the suffering, the brokenness in the world until our teens or even later. For others, The Wilderness is there from birth.

The first stage of every path to Making Good is recognizing and acknowledging a problem. In our hundreds of interviews with people sorting through the complex emotions this stage brings up, self-doubt was one of the most significant barriers to moving forward. They had identified a problem (or 20), but they just weren't sure what they could do about it, where they could start. It was a combination stemming from a lack of direction and that feeling of being stuck.

There was a pressure to get more credentials, to look older, or to pay more dues. Our families and parents often had different ideas of success, and for a lot of the people we talked to, it was this discord that became a real factor that ended up sending them back into that stuck feeling. How did their passions fit with the definitions of success their families held for them?

This is where so many of you are—looking for a path to somewhere meaningful. It's scary, but exciting too. You've begun an adventure, going after something ambitious in its potential impact on the world. But reassuring habits and traditions die hard, the threat of disappointment and failure can be paralyzing, and above all, the financial uncertainty of trying something untested is a risk many of us are afraid we can't afford. So how do we find the courage to invent a path that is unpredictable and hard to explain, when the people around us and our learned experiences often encourage us to submit to something more familiar?

The first step is realizing we are in The Wilderness and that it is okay. Then we need to name what's stopping us. Some of the challenges in heading down this new path are unique to our lives, others are things everyone struggles with at some point. Many are built into the structure of our society and are barriers that we often share with people of the same class, race, gender, sexual orientation, or educational background. There are psychological hang-ups we each have, different specific ways in which we feel stuck. It's important for us personally and collectively to acknowledge these disparities and recognize that overcoming them isn't easy. For every inspiring story we could tell you about someone overcoming oppression and a lack of opportunity, there are 10 stories of people who didn't make it through, couldn't launch the project they dreamed up.

Do you know what it is that's holding you up?

Have you ever said it out loud?

It's tempting to cling to our barriers and obstacles when we feel like giving up. There's a distinct comfort in victimhood—you don't have to risk anything, people extend you sympathy, and you get to feel the private satisfaction of being right when someone does you wrong. It's like shutting off the alarm on a cold morning and drifting back to sleep. Except all our options shut down. We surrender our power. Some of our excitement, our spark, our capacity to do something meaningful in our short time on earth slip away.

Dev

Even though I'm well into my career, that feeling of being in The Wilderness still recurs for me from time to time, especially when transitions make me feel like I'm at the beginning again. It isn't an exciting kind of unpredictability; it's straight-up scary. A couple of years into DreamNow, we had created Continuum, a service that provided follow-up for conferences. At first it was running like a business and earning money that supported the charity and a staff. But then we had a few bad months, lost a couple of key contracts, and ran into some unexpected problems with the technology we were using.

We ended up a nauseating 50 thousand dollars in the hole. It was the beginning of the recession, and I didn't know what to do. I got in the habit of phoning my parents and sort of baiting them with how hard it was to do what I was trying to do in this climate. "You're right," they'd say. "It is hard. You're trying everything you can. Take the day off and do something to treat yourself."

Then one day I nudged my brother for the same shoulder to cry on, and he just called everything I complained about an excuse. He began almost yelling at me, telling me to stop moping around. If I wanted to do it, do it. I tried to explain that he didn't understand the industry, my situation, the real-world reasons why fundraising wasn't in my control, but being the stubborn little brother, he hung up before I could finish.

Initially, I wasn't sure if he had a point at all. But something had shifted inside me. He'd inadvertently introduced a "what if" in my mind. What if my barriers *were* just excuses? What would I do if everything I was using to justify taking the day off wasn't true? I stayed up the night and drafted a plan, rethought who and how I was asking for money, and picked up the phone the next morning.

Within 2 months and after a lot of hard work, I found the confidence to find my way out of The Wilderness and I managed to raise close to $100,000. Once I was back on track, I realized that during my low period, I had stopped making calls and putting in the hours because I had convinced myself there wasn't any point.

We don't control the broader economy, and we often don't control the facts of our lives, but we can always control our response to them. That response is where our power lies, and to leverage it, we need to be conscious of our perspective. Our perspective on the world has immense power over our state of mind, just as the media's perspective has a profound impact on society.

We are actually capable of seeing things differently if we try. Instead of fixating on the power we don't have and how dire our circumstances are, we can look for possibility and hope. Each time we shift our perspective in this way, we lay down the tracks of new habits, building new muscles, increasing our willpower and range of choice.

In the end, we are the producer, the author, and the narrator of our personal story. We tell ourselves a story about who we are today and where we want to be someday. Both are creations of our mind, and the gap between how we see ourselves today and how we want to see ourselves is the path we need to travel to build a meaningful career.

The people we talked with who felt the most successful were those who saw the journey from current self to future self as filled with challenges to be conquered. The people who told us they felt stuck or were pessimistic about their chances of building a life and career of meaning presented similar challenges they'd faced as excuses to give up.

The path that Rebuilders are on is a nonlinear track that introduces career freedom, variety, and opportunity custom-cut to your abilities. On the mapless road, each episode offers new skills, challenges, and contacts that will contain a clue to the next episode.

One summer afternoon in Toronto, Dev sat in his office with his friend Kate Jongbloed, talking about the self-doubt that came up for her at the prospect of launching into a nonlinear career. She had recently returned from a summer in Ethiopia and was coming to the end of her international development degree at the University of Toronto. She talked about wrestling all her experiences and the events and people in her life into a sensible structure that would look like a career.

At the time, one whole wall in Dev's office was completely blank. DreamNow had just won a sponsorship from Post-it, so there were boxes and boxes of the pastel square pads lying around. Inspired, Dev and his friend started writing all of their life experiences down on stickies and putting them on the wall, making maps of their lives—different experiences, turning points, people they met who changed their direction. Just getting it on the wall enabled them to see and understand their own and each other's maps in a new way.

Patterns emerged. Looking at Kate's map, it was obvious that global health and HIV/AIDS awareness work were abiding passions of hers, and she had written five stickies about writing and blogging. After seeing all of her interests and ideas together, it was easy for Kate to make the connections. It enabled her to start to make a real plan, to start to push past the uncertainty she felt, and to pick just one thing to begin working on—blogging. A few years later, she has found a job that pays her to be a blogger on issues surrounding women and girls, while she completes a graduate program at the school of population and public health at the University of British Columbia. The stickies on the wall are beginning to come together.

We can rarely feel the connection of one moment to another while we're living it, but with a little perspective, we come to see the inspiration and causation that propel us forward. The truth is you don't begin your career at one particular time. Everything that you have done to get to this point—what you have learned, the people you have met, your time off, your work experience—has brought you here. Even people in the most traditional fields will credit their success to unplanned turns, to ideas that surprised them. You have to trust that doing good work and doing it earnestly will carry you from one sustaining project to the next, that just because there's no corporate ladder to ascend doesn't mean there's no future work for you. The skills and experiences you pick up along the way only make you more prepared for the next challenge you'll face, and the path that evolves to carry you through will indeed be a path—a nonlinear career path.

We face self-doubt and confusion all the time, no matter what we have accomplished in the past or how confident we seem to others, but realizing we always have the ability to change is what gives us the grounded self-assurance we need to walk this path. It's a path, not a career—it's about the constantly evolving now.

STAGE 2: FINDING YOUR SPECIAL POWERS

Magazine profiles of the most creative, the most powerful, the most up-and-coming movers and shakers can give us the impression that life just feels different for really successful people. Sometimes what we read about them seems to suggest that they've always had a clear path, one step after another, all stemming from some grand epiphany where they felt *chosen* for their work. It was as if they were clueless and then one morning they had this experience and, boom, there it was, their life's purpose clear as daylight, driving them straight toward the magazine on the kitchen table.

Thinking this way can make us feel like if we haven't been *discovered,* then we probably aren't worthy of great things. But when you talk to people who have achieved a level of success, you find out they, too, are caught up in that long, unfolding process of figuring out who they are, what they know and don't know, and how to get paid. The truth is that neat epiphanies rarely actually occur.

The path to success isn't as clear-cut as it may sound in the magazines. When a story is written about what you're working on one day, it will be abbreviated, summarized, and centered around a point from where it all began—even though your work will be a much more gradual process.

The second stage is about finding your edge, the special power that we all possess. We start the search by looking back at the experiences that have gotten us here today. By looking back, you can begin to uncover a story, your story, and find out that you actually do have a unique edge, in spite of a nagging insecurity about not being good enough, not being ready enough. The feeling may be tied to a cultural phenomenon going on with people in their twenties and thirties today—a stage the *New York Times* has termed "Emerging Adulthood." Emerging Adulthood suggests that today's young people get stunted after college, that we get caught in a protracted period of nomadic identity-seeking, trying things out but not settling down, and our uncertainty can contribute to our feeling that we're not cut out for anything yet.

But what we need to understand is that in spite of that feeling, we are already in the middle of the work that we need to do. We are already living our "real" lives.

We have been making choices for our whole lives—whether we are aware of it or not. In fact, all of the choices that you have made up until this point have brought you to the point where you are reading this book and acknowledging that you want to do something that enables you to make money and change the world. You aren't at the beginning—you are already in the middle. You are the perfect person to make the next move. If you are waiting for a moment to start, if you are waiting for some sort of signal to tell you that you can begin, you are missing out on what is happening right now.

Marisol Becerra is the perfect example of someone who woke up to the middle of her path. She was living on the west side of Chicago in a neighborhood called Little Village when she and Billy first met. La Villita, as she calls it, is what you might call a depressed neighborhood. It's filled with vacant lots, empty storefronts, and plenty of poverty. Gangs like the Latin Kings and Two Six control the neighborhood, selling drugs and instilling fear in local residents, while dominating the one green space in the neighborhood, Piotrowski Park. Like many low-income communities, Little Village is surrounded on all sides by polluters. Within a 10-block radius, there is a plastics manufacturing plant, a steel drum reprocessing plant, a scrap metal recycling plant, a coal-fired power plant, and a garbage transfer station.The factories and the vehicles that go in and out of them create air, water, and noise pollution that are a gross injustice to the residents of Little Village. So who would you expect to play a leading role in fighting the polluters? Local lawyers? Business owners? Politicians?

In fact, one of the leading activists in Little Village for the past five years has been Marisol, a student at DePaul University, as well as a recipient of a Brower Youth Award for young environmental leaders.

Her unlikely path to leadership began one Saturday afternoon, when her mother asked if she wanted to join her for a leadership training sponsored by a local environmental justice organization. Marisol didn't have anything better to do. The training began with a "toxic tour" of her neighborhood, from polluting plant to polluting plant, with details on the toxins each released and the impacts on human health. The last stop was the biggest plant of all, the biggest polluter in all of Chicago—and just a few blocks from her house—the Crawford coal-fired power plant. As a child, she'd noticed the constant stream of smoke visible from her window and thought it was a cloud factory.

The tour guide mentioned a recent Harvard study that found that the Crawford plant caused 26 deaths, 350 emergency room visits, and 1,800 asthma attacks each year in the area. Those statistics resonated with Marisol. Her mother, who had been healthy prior to coming to the United States from Mexico, was experiencing respiratory problems. Her sister developed asthma when she was 3. Learning about the possible source of these ailments made her angry. "I knew I wasn't the only one in my community who didn't know these things," she told me. "I hadn't really ever been outside Little Village, but I began to explore the north side of Chicago for the first time. I saw a better quality of life, but one my community couldn't afford. I decided to do something."

She started by volunteering with the Little Village Environmental Justice Organization, the group that put on the leadership training, helping with little things—stuffing envelopes, answering phones. Marisol loves talking, debating, getting into it with family and friends, and she realized that if the organization needed someone to convince people, she could do it. Pretty soon she was going door to door in her community. She then helped create a youth group to engage more young people in the community and started a newsletter, *El Cilantro*—"that extra something in Mexican dishes that just makes them super yummy"—to spread the word.

Things really started to take off in her sophomore year of high school when the organization began a community mapping project. She'd always liked media, especially taking pictures and recording video, but she was an amateur. She found a summer program that trained youth on using media for social change, and in it, she created a documentary to tell her community's story. When she was introduced to Google Maps, it all came together. Working with other youth in her group, she filled out the map with pictures, videos, and stories, and the organization made it a centerpiece of its campaign to shut down the Crawford plant. After pressure from Marisol's group and others throughout Chicago and Illinois, the governor signed an order to reduce mercury emissions in the state by 90 percent, which will require the plant to choose between expensive pollution control upgrades or closure.

Marisol's activism has opened up the world to her—scholarships, global travel, and a coveted White House internship—but that's not the point. Marisol's story isn't over; it's evolving. She's got her whole life ahead of her. Who would have thought that a 16-year-old girl was the ideal candidate to fight huge corporations polluting the city of Chicago? As it turned out, this outgoing, computer-savvy, Spanish-speaking teen was perfect. In a neighborhood where over half the population is under 21, she was able to raise awareness and organize people in a way few others could. She didn't have all the skills she'd needed, but she was more prepared than she thought.

Looking back, it's easy to connect the dots. Of course Marisol was the right person for that moment. But at the beginning, there was no way to know. She certainly didn't.

So what are you in the middle of?

What might you be the perfect person for, at this very moment?

STAGE 3: THE KIN

From a very early age, we all have a deep craving to belong. Throughout most of human evolution, we lived in small groups of between a few dozen and several thousand people. In the early 1990s, a British anthropologist named Robin Dunbar conducted a massive survey of the size of human groupings throughout recorded history and noticed a pattern: From the size of ancient hunter-gatherer and farming communities to the basic military unit size of Roman and modern armies, the number 150 kept coming up. In groups that grew beyond 150, social cohesion broke down and groups began to split. Researchers since have suggested that "Dunbar's Number" can be stretched to 200 or even 300, but communities growing too far beyond that can't maintain strong social bonds or trust.

Today we all live with a confusingly dichotomous relationship to community. Increasingly, our home lives are places of isolation—"nuclear family" units separated by walls and fences and yards that are rarely crossed. We have meals alone, or together, facing the TV. One of the reasons so many people remember college as some of the best years of their lives is because they're the only years we live like we evolved to live, in close proximity to lots of other people. As our friend Bill McKibben says, the irony is that one of the goals of college is to help you make enough money that you never have to live that way again.

At the same time, the social pressure to build online networks of friends, followers, and fans plunges us into a vast virtual community that starves us of the kind of genuine human connection that can actually sustain us. In Japan, the New Year's moment is celebrated by hundreds of thousands not with a kiss or jump or "kampai" (cheers) with friends, but with a mass tweet, smashing global "tweet-per-second" records. The ability to touch hundreds, or thousands, at a time scratches the basic human itch to connect, to be in community, but only for a second, and the rewards are shallow and often leave you feeling empty and alone. One of Billy's friends told us that the day she reached her 1,000th Facebook friend was at a time when she was feeling more isolated and lonely than she had in years.

Study after study shows that we're happier when we're together, but sometimes it can be hard to find your people, your tribe, your community. Maybe your family and the community you grew up in don't seem to support the values or passion you hold dear. Schools and work environments are too often designed for competition, not connection and collaboration, breeding a cliquish and alienating environment. It's apparent by simply noticing all the ways in which marketers suggest we can be part of a club or a movement, just by buying their products. And evangelical churches, sensitive to the absence of reliable, genuine communities in our culture, offer their members an inclusive warmth that keeps seats filled week after week.

Fortunately, the support we all need can be just a call, click, or coffee shop away. Most of us start off into The Wilderness with just one or a few friends who understand what we're going through. We have late-night conversations and long walks to make sense of all the confusing things. We become stronger as we accumulate more friends. So the question is: How do we find our people?

HOW TO FIND YOUR PEOPLE

There are hundreds of ways to find larger groups of people with shared values and purpose. Here's a starter list of three quick ways to get you into your community:

* **Take the online offline.** There are online networks and organizations for almost every interest. It's great to be involved in these sites and networks, but look for opportunities to take the online networking offline as fast as you can. Go to bar nights, potlucks, film screenings, conferences, community association meetings, or open houses of these networks with the goal of finding just one other simpatico person to come to future events with you.

* **Bring it to your town.** Look for events that are going on in other towns or cities that attract the people that you want to be hanging out with. Contact the organizer or host organization and sign up to be a local organizer or part of the team that is bringing it to your community. You now have permission to get in touch with as many people as you can and have an organization offering you some support to get started. Whether it is a TEDx event, ChangeCamp, or a Meetup Everywhere–empowered event, there are great opportunities to get to know people. You don't even have to be the host if you aren't the gregarious type; all events need people behind the scenes, and often, being on the organizing team can give you a real chance to build long-term relationships with your teammates.

* **Network across.** Often when people network, they look for people who have the answers to the questions or resources they need. Look across instead—ask people you admire for references to people who have asked them similar questions. Ask for an introduction—people are usually willing to introduce you to someone asking a similar question, and they may have even found the answers you've been looking for.

When you do find true community, it can feel like a homecoming, like the discovery of a new family you didn't know but was there all along. In these communities, you will find friendship, comradeship, and a kind of unity of purpose. These are the people who will drop everything to help when you're in need, with whom you can share some laughs and commiseration when choices seem unknown. Your community is made up of those who will help you land a job when you're broke, partner with you when you want to launch a new company, or at least have a drink with you on a patio.

In Chapter 6, we'll dig into some strategies for growing and maintaining a network that actually has the strength and trust to deliver these things. Before long, if you're not there already, you'll end up being a part of multiple communities based around workplaces, conferences, Listservs, and who knows what else. For now, consider that you are already part of a broad movement of Rebuilders, and you aren't doing it alone. Your community is actually *everywhere*. There's a growing acceptance of this trackless track and more and more people that can help you bridge between the different steps on our nonlinear paths.

STAGE 4: THE TESTS

As we find our edge, discover our communities, and accept the path we have begun to walk down, we need to stop and look around. It takes confidence to know that feeling on the edge of control is actually the feeling of being on the right path. You are figuring out how to live your purpose and living it at the same time. Stage 4 is about finding yourself in those moments when things feel like they are in chaos and learning to take a deep breath and find that personal power inside to get up, get out, and carry on.

Billy

In November 2007, the Energy Action Coalition organized Power Shift '07, the first-ever national youth climate summit in the United States. Over 6,000 young climate leaders from across the country gathered in Washington, DC, to lobby Congress on the most critical threat of our times.

One of the culminating events of Power Shift involved testimony before the House Select Committee for Energy Independence and Global Warming. This was our generation's first chance to have our ideas and grievances etched into the Congressional Record. I had worked with Chairman Ed Markey to put together a diverse group of youth leaders from across the country—an indigenous woman talking about the impacts of global warming and oil drilling in Alaska, a Hurricane Katrina survivor and activist, another from a coal-mining community in Tennessee, and a young man promoting solar energy in California. Chairman Markey asked me to be on the panel as well to represent the youth climate movement.

As coordinator of the coalition, I had worked for years to get to this moment. Power Shift had been a huge success, and here I was getting ready to testify before Congress—except, I felt like crap. I'd barely slept the past week, and that morning, I was running around Capitol Hill ensuring that the green hard hats we'd ordered arrived in time for our rally on the steps of the Capitol. On top of that, public speaking was one of my biggest fears, a fact that may or may not trace back to a traumatizing Christmas pageant performance during middle school. I don't really want to talk about it.

I peeked into the massive hearing room. It was packed, the most full it had been in decades, according to one of Congressman Markey's aides. Ten minutes to start and I could feel my stomach tighten and my mouth dry up. I ran to the bathroom to collect myself and looked into the mirror.

These are our moments of truth—a time to conquer our fears and find the power within us to overcome the obstacles we face, regardless of how overwhelming they may feel. At certain moments in all of our lives, we are called to lead.

When the dreams we have for ourselves match the reality of our experience, we're living our purpose. These moments of leadership aren't always about being in the spotlight. They aren't always about presenting to thousands or asking for millions of dollars. They are often quiet moments as we are getting dressed to leave or are making notes in preparation for a call. We know that what we are doing is right, but it feels so uncomfortable that all we want is for someone to come down from above to answer our hesitant wondering about whether we're doing the right thing with a confident *Yes*.

Even though Dev has been to countless conferences and in rooms with all sorts of intimidating people, during that first moment when he enters a crowded room of strangers, doubt still creeps in. Even though he knows breaking the ice with a single person will make it all easier, he gets hung up on whom to approach, what to say, and how he'll feel if they ignore him. The feeling is irrational, but the fear is real.

The confidence to know you can handle those moments isn't something that people are born with; it is a quality that has to be renewed each time you find yourself wondering whether to step forward or step back. But that's what a mantra is for.

Billy

At the first five-day retreat for the Rockwood Leadership Program, Robert, our facilitator, gave the 24 of us some time to ourselves to take a first stab at a short and simple phrase that would remind us of our purpose and ground us in our power.

He said we would have to test it out on the full group, and we all moved to different parts of the room.

I sat on the ground with my back against the wall, hoping that something would come to me before I had to say it aloud to 24 of the most influential nonprofit leaders I'd ever met. A phrase that had been in my head for the past few weeks popped up: "Nothing to it but to do it." It seemed almost too stupid to use, but I couldn't ignore the little burst of energy it gave me. There was a confidence in it. That's it, I thought. Done. Nothing to it but to do it. Looking around the room at everyone scribbling notes, pacing, mumbling words, I think I was the first in the group to settle on one.

After a little more time, Robert called us back together into a standing circle. We each had to repeat our phrase three times to the group, with a deep breath in between each repetition, and everyone else would react based on how authentic it seemed, how much it seemed to give power and purpose to the person speaking it. But this was the catch: We had to keep trying if we didn't get it right. A few nailed it on the first try— raucous applause and whooping would follow the three repetitions. And some never got it right that day—some tepid applause and lots of love but no affirmation of the mantra, after five, six, even ten tries.

I was somewhere in between. The first try got a good response but not enough to move on to the next person. Robert suggested I add a pause between the two phrases—"nothing to it" . . . "but to do it." That helped. There were actually two key ideas in the phrase: I was ready for whatever I needed to do *and* I needed to get out there and do it. Nevertheless, not being much of a performer, and still working out the kinks, after three attempts, I got a pretty good cheer and was relieved when Robert moved on to the next person in the circle.

I've used my mantra almost every day since, but it has evolved several times into a fuller reflection of my personal power. In its current form (as of this writing), it is: "I am part of the beloved community. Building a more just and sustainable world—for my family, my community, and all of creation. I am ready to follow. I am ready to lead. Nothing to it but to do it."

These few sentences do a lot for me: They connect me, ground me in my purpose, and give me confidence to do whatever I need to do. If I'm feeling alienated from a person or group of people, the "I am part of the beloved community" can reconnect me. If I'm deciding on whether to take on a project or make a hard decision, the second sentence, "building a more just and sustainable world—for my family, my community, and all of creation," clarifies my purpose and priorities. The "ready to follow, ready to lead" bit reminds me that the best leadership is subtle and often comes from behind, only vocal at key moments. The last piece, the original root of my mantra, helps me finish that last set of push-ups, jump into a cold lake for a swim, or start speaking in front of big groups.

Sitting in a bathroom stall minutes before representing the 6,000 young people that had come to DC to lobby Congress, I felt dread. I grabbed the sink and looked in the mirror. I took a deep breath. Without thinking, I started to repeat my mantra, "I am part of the beloved community . . . " I'd been saying it for months, connected with deep breaths, and it had become second nature. I left the bathroom feeling electric and walked the halls outside the room, repeating it over and over, with some scattered deep ommmms. Passersby looked at me like I was crazy and kept their distance, but I didn't care. As I walked into the room, I was feeling confident, powerful, and excited for this opportunity to speak for my generation. You can see the results on YouTube.

DAILY PRACTICE #2: INNER POWER

Now it's your turn. Take a minute to think about a time when you felt in control, when you felt your most powerful, the fullest version of yourself today. Maybe you were doing exactly what you knew you had to do, or maybe it was crossing the finish line on a project that you had put your best work into. Who was around you? How did your body feel? What were you doing?

> Place yourself there. Put the book down while you close your eyes and think about how you felt in that moment.

> What does it feel like to remember that moment? Could you feel a surge of energy? Did you smile?

A mantra can capture that feeling, trick your brain into producing the chemicals you need to overcome a difficult situation. It can remind you of what's important and who you are.

This is a good discipline to work on with a friend you trust, or a small group of such friends, but it's also fine to do it on your own. The mantra you are going to develop is a simple phrase that expresses your purpose and your source of power. It will ground you, it will help give you the confidence to step into the unknown as you pursue your new path. It may take you only a few minutes to find the words, but more likely, it will evolve and change over your lifetime.

STEP 1: CHOOSE THE WORDS

Find a place that is both quiet and comfortable. Write a statement that expresses who you are, that connects you to your inner sense of power. It should always be stated in the positive—what you want, not what you don't want. It can be a couple of sentences, a simple phrase, or even a single word.

STEP 2: FOCUS IT

Work to remove all of the unnecessary words. Every word and every punctuation mark should be there for a reason. Say the full mantra out loud three times, repeating it louder each time.

> How do you feel?
>
> Do you feel a sense of confidence, a feeling of power?
>
> Or are you forcing it?
>
> It's okay if it doesn't feel right immediately—keep working to find the words and phrases that fit and excite you.

STEP 3: MAKE IT PART OF YOUR ROUTINE

Once you have a mantra that you feel is right, it's time to put it to use. For the first few weeks, try to use it at least 10 to 15 times a day. Put a Post-it note on your computer or desk, set up alerts on your calendar, or do whatever method works to remind you. When you wake up in the morning, before getting out of bed, making an important phone call, working out, or facing a decision you have to make about your own life, speak your mantra three times, silently or out loud. Each time you say your phrase, take a deep breath and anchor yourself in that feeling of excitement, in that smile, and in your sense of inner power.

CHAPTER 3

THE OPPORTUNITIES

*"You never change things by fighting the existing
reality. To change something build a new model that
makes the existing model obsolete."*
—BUCKMINSTER FULLER

If you zoomed in for a close look at North America's current infrastructure, you'd be excused for thinking we were living on the site of an archaeological dig. The electrical grids that transport electricity from power plants to our homes were mostly built in the Roaring Twenties. Our passenger rail system has become a tourist's indulgence, good for chugging along to enjoy the scenic route but slow, unreliable, and, in many cases, unaffordable for regular commuting. We spend enormous sums every year on roads that crumble from weather and heavy use faster than we can fix them. Our buildings are some of the least efficient in the world, burning up fuel, electricity, and countless dollars for homeowners and business owners. After a 2009 review of American infrastructure, the American Society of Civil Engineers assigned an overall grade to the drinking water, schools, roads, parks, and waste systems: an ominous D.

But it's not just hard infrastructure; virtually every current system that supports our daily lives—healthcare, banking, energy, food, you name it—was created decades, sometimes centuries, ago and hasn't been updated to account for so many developments in the modern world: increasing population, new technologies, an evolving understanding of sustainability, and, a big one, the Internet. The business models of most firms in almost every sector of the economy are now broken. The existing corporations that dominate those sectors aren't inherently good or evil. They provide critical goods and services humans enjoy around the planet, and their sponsorships support many important projects in the arts, schools, and the nonprofit sector. But we need a better set of rules governing their behavior.

But we also just need new and improved business models, and outsiders are often the perfect people for the job. Sean Parker didn't have to be a musician to appreciate how Napster, his first effort to enable open access to music on the Web, fundamentally altered the economics of the music industry. The addition of MySpace, Etsy, Kickstarter, and hundreds of other social, Web-enabled platforms and games have enabled millions of creative people to make a living making beautiful things.

But rebuilding doesn't just mean starting a company; it can happen in every form of organization—nonprofits, political leagues, foundations, cooperatives, LC3s, and partnerships—and every sort of hybrid. The systems these entities are displacing represent most of the job and work opportunities out there. Disruption can and will employ most of us. It's where many of tomorrow's jobs will be found.

To understand how and where to find disruptive opportunities, it's imperative to understand a bit about the history behind each of these systems, to try to discern the original logic in their design and the points at which that logic started to peel apart from the needs of the changing world. Most of these systems, when we really look, arose as by-products of a long series of accidents. At some point, there was a problem, and someone solved it. The innovation spread, built power around it, and calcified, even as the problem itself grew and shifted out of the original solution's grasp.

As the influential conservative economist Milton Friedman wrote: "There is enormous inertia—a tyranny of the status quo—in private and especially governmental arrangements. Only a crisis—actual or perceived—produces real change. When that crisis occurs, the actions that are taken depend on the ideas that are lying around. That, I believe, is our basic function: to develop alternatives to existing policies, to keep them alive and available until the politically impossible becomes politically inevitable."

The crises—social, economic, and ecological—that make large-scale change inevitable are coming faster and faster. Many of the basic systems that undergird our society are clearly already at a breaking point. The statistics are overwhelming.

* 1.1 billion people don't have access to clean water[1]

* 75 percent of global fisheries are at or beyond capacity[2]

[1] UNEP (2008), "Vital Water Graphics—An Overview of the State of the World's Fresh and Marine Waters." 2nd Edition. UNEP, Nairobi, Kenya.

[2] Food and Agriculture Organization. "State of the World Fisheries and Aquaculture." 2002.

* 80 percent of the world's original forests are gone[3]

* 99 percent of the stuff bought in North America is thrown in the trash within 6 months of purchasing[4]

* 1.3 billion tons of food are wasted or lost each year, which is equivalent to a third of all the food produced each year[5]

We really do have the intelligence and imagination necessary to make these systems work much, much better. Consider this: Thanks to research and development and the race to innovate in the IT sector, we are all walking around with computers in our mobile devices that are a hundred times smaller, a thousand times faster, and a million times cheaper than the original computers. If the exponential pace of development that has taken place in the tech sector were applied to other sectors, a plane traveling from New York to Paris that took 7 hours and cost $900 in 1978 (in 2010 dollars) would now take less than 0.25 seconds and cost less than a penny.

Today every system can be rebuilt in a way that actually makes sense for people, for profit, and for the world. This rebuilding, this reassembling of the pieces that we have access to today is the answer to making money and changing the world. Each of the areas is sufficiently large that the rebuilding and maintenance of the systems could each create tens of millions of jobs all around the world. Rebuilding is about action. Work.

[3] World Resources Institute. "Forest Landscapes Initiative." www.wri.org/project/global-forest-watch (this is an ongoing tracking site)

[4] Leonard, Annie. *Story of Stuff.* 2007. www.storyofstuff.org

[5] Gostavasson, Jenny, Christel Cederberg, and Ulf Sonesson. *Global Food Losses and Food Waste.* Rep. Rome: FAO, 2011.

The scale of the transformation required is daunting but shouldn't be seen as an insurmountable hurdle. Society has achieved massive transformations before. Many countries around the world have actually substantially made some of the core system–shifting transformations we need here. Costa Rica is 99 percent powered by clean energy. Israel is the most water-efficient country in the world, reusing 74 percent. Thailand's unemployment rate is around 1 percent. And sometimes we have real help from our governments. Consider how Germany built one of the strongest clean energy industries in the world with smart policies or how the US military funded and even developed internally many of the major telecommunication and semiconductor breakthroughs in the '60s that brought us the Internet.

And here's the really beautiful advantage we have, one that is only recently beginning to be widely understood: Rebuilding one system makes it easier to rebuild the others. When we rebuild our energy system to expand affordable clean energy all over the world, we can purify clean water, improve public health, and more easily bring Internet to rural areas. When we improve our education system, society will have better innovators, problem solvers, and engaged citizens in every sector of the economy.

Some of the changes will take generations to accomplish, providing good and meaningful work to people along the way in every community, all around the world. We each have important ways to contribute in all areas of our lives. As eaters, shoppers, workers, or parents, we can be part of bringing humanity back into harmony with each other and the planet. This work is going to take millions of individual acts of guts and ingenuity, millions of people joining the movement as individuals and workers aligned in purpose. As *Time* Senior Editor Lev Grossman wrote in his 2006 cover story awarding Person of the Year to *You*, "It's about the many wresting power from the few and helping one another for nothing and how that will not only change the world, but also change the way the world changes." You're reading this book because you sense that something is deeply wrong, and you know there has to be possibilities for better, smarter, more sustainable redesign everywhere. This is where they are.

The opportunities are everywhere across the spectrum of industries, all waiting to reward your creativity and hard work. In this chapter, we'll check out many of the systems currently in crisis to determine where they've run aground, show you some of the work currently underway to create positive change, and leave you with the questions you need to ask to rethink the industry that interests you. Today every system can be rebuilt in a way that makes good in the world, and there is work to do because of it. This is about training ourselves to see opportunity in apparent chaos, to use our understanding of fundamental human needs to create brand-new solutions that are both good for our world and for ourselves.

INFORMATION TECHNOLOGY: THE NETWORK OF NETWORKS

Before Google was a pixel on the screens of Sergey Brin and Larry Page, Gordon Moore was one of the original "tech entrepreneurs." Three years before founding Intel, when Moore was still research director at the Fairchild Semiconductor Laboratory, he noticed an amazing pattern. The number of transistors in an integrated circuit (essentially the processing power of computers) had doubled every year from 1958 to 1965. In a famous article in the April 19, 1965, issue of *Electronics* magazine, Moore predicted that the trend would continue for at least 10 years. "Moore's Law" has been refined to a doubling every 18 months to 2 years and has predicted with remarkable accuracy the exponential improvements in computer technology over nearly 50 years.

Faster computers have enabled technological progress in virtually every industry. Advances in engineering, math, sciences, and dozens of other fields are made possible by the powerful analytic tools computers provide. Many other technologies seem to be following the same "Moore's Law" cost curve as computers. Solar cells and fiber optics, the so called "tubes" through which our data and communications flow, are all cutting costs and increasing efficiencies at blinding speed.

Combine the three—supercomputing processor power, communication at the speed of light, and abundant clean energy—and add software platforms (Facebook, Twitter, and Wikipedia) that facilitate real-time knowledge sharing across the entire planet, and we have, well, superhuman powers. We have infinite knowledge, everlasting energy, a face-to-face conversation with teammates in Singapore and Cairo at the speed of light. The potential of collective human intelligence enabled by this network of networks is underwriting change in all of the industries that are being rebuilt today.

While many companies, organizations, and governments have their own in-house research and development staff, they are beginning to turn to us, "the crowd," for some of their toughest challenges. InnoCentive, an "open innovation company," partners with institutions to offer cash awards for the best solutions to R&D challenges from engineering to computer science to chemistry. Over 1,000 challenges have been solved by over 250,000 solvers all over the world.

In late 2010, NASA posted a challenge titled "forecasting solar particle events." Large bursts of energy from the sun was a risk for astronauts and satellites, and for years, NASA had been working to improve its models that predicted when the bursts would come. Their best models were only 50 percent accurate and gave only 4 hours notice. Within days, hundreds of solvers had signed up to work on the problem, and when they surveyed the submissions after 90 days, they found that a retired scientist and amateur ham radio operator had developed models that were 85 percent accurate and doubled lead time to 8 hours.

Internet-based technologies also enable a scaling up of democracy the Greeks could only have dreamed of. One of Billy's longtime collaborators in the Energy Action Coalition, Jared Duval, wrote a book called *Next Generation Democracy*, which shows how a range of new, Web-enabled tools, combined with a newly global, progressive, and tech-savvy generation, is poised to change the world. The ability to inform, test preferences, organize coherent dialogue among millions, and make collective decisions is now a reality.

Various experiments are scaling true democracy to meet our growing population density and complexity. A nonprofit called America Speaks used "21st-century town halls" with tens of thousands of New Orleans residents and survivors of Katrina to plan for the rebuilding there. These town halls are now being used across the country to bring true public dialogue and debate to solve tough problems. Governments are using technology to take dramatic steps toward transparency. Beth Noveck was appointed to lead the Open Government Initiative, a commitment to greater transparency in government than ever before. Through data.gov, Beth and her team created access for analysts, app creators, and just regular folks to understand and actually work with their government, a pretty radical concept if you think about it.

We start with IT because it undergirds the advances in virtually every sector of the economy—and certainly each of the ones we explore below. But also like the others below, it has the opportunity to be rebuilt itself. Many of the technologies and devices that we use remain highly toxic, unaffordable to the bulk of humanity, and represent one of the fastest-growing shares of global carbon pollution. The Internet may send all of our data to the "Cloud," but the reality is that there are thousands of data centers on land filled with servers that take energy to run. In 2009, these data centers used 2 percent of all US power—more than all color TVs combined.[6]

Greening IT, a free e-book developed by dozens of engineers and global thought leaders and released under creative commons license, is a great primer on some of the solutions available, required reading for anyone focused on a career in this sector. Innovators will be using new network technology for good work in all sectors as well as reengineering and creating new and improved hardware that's cheaper, lasts longer, and is fully recyclable. The very nature of IT has been that reinvention is hardwired into the design of the industry. There is an opportunity to shift this reinvention in a more sustainable direction.

[6] Jonathan Koomey. 2011. "Growth in data center electricity use 2005 to 2010." Oakland, CA: Analytics Press. August 1.

ENERGY: THE HANGING SOLAR GARDENS
OF BLACK MESA

In 1712, an English blacksmith and lay preacher named Thomas Newcomen invented something he called the atmospheric engine. Relatively inefficient at first, the machine worked by burning coal to generate steam, condensing that steam to move a lever that pumped water out of flooded tin mines, allowing minerals to be mined at much greater depths. Thanks to the advent of Newcomen's "steam engine," a simple lump of coal came to replace a team of 100 horses, enabling more work at a faster pace than had ever been possible before.

In physics, energy is defined as the capacity for doing work: If we want work done, we need energy to make it happen. Fossil fuels, particularly coal, gas, and oil, store lots of potential work in very small packages that are easily opened, and they're relatively cheap to collect and store. Cheap and abundant fossil energy has fueled exponential increases in material wealth, life expectancy, technological innovation, agricultural productivity, and human population. After remaining flat for a millennium, per capita income in the West rose by an average of 20 percent in the 1700s, 200 percent in the 1800s, and 740 percent in the past century.

This single energy innovation that allowed fossil energy to power machines was a catalyst for the Industrial Revolution, put a man on the moon, gave rise to the professions and large-scale manufacturing (not to mention toasters, refrigerators, and many of the other conveniences and mini-miracles of modern life). The later advances from people like Thomas Edison, Benjamin Franklin, and Nicola Tesla wouldn't have been possible without these earlier breakthroughs, and the Western way of life has become utterly dependent on oil for transportation, agriculture, plastics, and chemicals.

So what would happen if we ran out of oil? Although noticing the impact today requires a little education and imagination, most independent analysts agree that global oil production peaked around 2005 and that supplies will not last long.[7] The dual forces of peak oil and climate change mean that oil is becoming more scarce and expensive, spiking the cost of virtually everything we eat, build, and consume.

Our fossil fuel energy regime is arguably the most destructive and certainly the most profitable industry in the history of the world. It's also one of the most centralized, controlled by a small number of multinational corporations that have invested trillions of dollars in unsustainable and outdated infrastructure like dirty coal-fired power plants, oil refineries, mines and wells, and pipes and transmission lines. These industries have every incentive to block or stall a transition that could make all those investments go bad. And they've spent hundreds of millions of dollars on PR campaigns, campaign contributions, and lobbying to do just that.

But against the odds, the tide turns. When Bill Gates was given an opportunity at the annual Technology, Entertainment, Design (TED) Conference in 2010 to share a wish with the influential TED community, he didn't emphasize the subjects he's best known for, his work at Microsoft or his philanthropic support of vaccines and seeds through the Gates Foundation. "If you gave me only one wish for the next 50 years," he said, "[it would be that] this thing that is half the cost of coal and doesn't

---

[7] Heinberg, Richard. *Peak Everything: Waking up to the Century of Declines.* Gabriola, BC: New Society, 2007.

emit CO_2 gets invented." To address poverty, improve standards of living, and protect the planet from climate destabilization, "this is the one with the greatest impact."

He continued: "We need lots of companies working on this. A lot of them you'll look at and say, 'they're crazy,' and that's good. There are now dozens of companies, we need it to be hundreds, who, if their science goes well, if the funding for their pilot plants goes well, that they can compete for this. And it's best if multiples succeed, because then you could use a mix of these things."

In 2008, global investors spent $250 billion building new energy capacity, and for the first time, the lion's share of that money went to renewable sources—$140 billion versus $110 billion for fossil fuel technologies.[7] Before long, the sheer number of new and improved green products and projects flooding the market will deflate the cost of clean energy to the point where going green saves people money. As this happens, newer technologies will make their predecessors obsolete.

But when you look at the time it took other disruptive technologies to become prevalent, even the mostly rapidly adopted ones—like radios, cell phones, color TVs, and computers—it just takes too long. Even with strong government support and smart policies, the inertia in our energy system will take a generation to fully overcome. We don't have that much time.

The next model of energy development is about new technologies, innovative financing, and smart policy, but the critical x factor is people like you. As small-scale clean energy technologies become cheaper than big expensive fossil energy projects, anyone can be a developer and owner in the new energy economy.

Billy

Some mornings, you can feel the earth shake under your feet. On the high mesas of the Navajo Reservation, my wife, Wahleah, and I are building a home for our family—just a few miles from a coal strip mine, once the largest in the world. For almost 40 years, Navajo coal has powered the air conditioners, the bright lights, and suburban sprawl of Phoenix, Las Vegas, and Los Angeles, but still more than half of the tribe's members don't have electricity or running water.

Though the Black Mesa Mine closed in 2005, its associated Kayenta Mine still sends coal to the Navajo Generating Station on the reservation near Page, Arizona. In addition to this and the open pit Navajo coal mine, the reservation hosts two of the region's three coal plants. The tribe owns none of these facilities, and though it receives royalties and tax revenue, it has no say in how they do business.

Wahleah grew up here, in the shadows of dynamite, razor-wire fences, and earth movers so big they make you feel like an ant. She's working with people to convert the mining lands into a series of large-scale solar projects that will provide jobs, power, and revenue for a community with over 70 percent unemployment. The community folks want to be able to graze their sheep and cattle on the land that was once theirs, so we had been looking for a technology that could be strung along lines, allowing the land to regenerate, grow grass, and support the livelihoods of community residents in many ways.

The vision for my company, Solar Mosaic, was inspired by Wahleah's work. To fully enable an energy 2.0 movement, we don't just need a breakthrough technology—we also need community organizers ready to take on the damaging energy systems in their own communities and an online platform to simplify and accelerate the solar development process. Mosaic employs an online marketplace that lets people post clean energy projects and mobilize communities of support to fund them. We built Mosaic to empower people to develop community clean energy at massive scale and to clean up and democratize our relationship to energy by enabling many more clean energy projects to find financing, allowing everyone to own a piece of the new energy economy.

Enough solar energy hits the Earth every 40 minutes to power humanity's energy needs for an entire year. The solar panel, in particular, is a game-changing invention—power at a human scale, directly from the sun, the original source of all of our energy. Place a solar panel in the sunlight and it starts creating energy. Attach it to the grid, use or sell the power, and you're instantly saving or even making money.

We need to rebuild our entire energy ecosystem: how we collect energy, store it, transmit it, consume it, and fund it. There's not a magic bullet that will fix everything. To replace the amount of work powered by fossil fuels and maintain a high quality of life for people around the world, we need lots of people, projects, and ideas. That's the good news. As we rebuild our energy ecosystem, there are endless career opportunities for entrepreneurs, academics, laborers, and safety experts.

Who is going to decommission and repurpose all of our existing fossil fuel energy infrastructure? Who will convert billions of gas-powered cars to run on sustainable biofuels or electric power? Who will design and manufacture the 8,000 different parts in a wind turbine? Who will install, maintain, repair, recycle, and upgrade the hundreds of millions of solar panels we'll need to accomplish a shift to 100 percent clean energy? People. With good-paying jobs. And behind each of these tasks, there are the transportation, accounting, management, and other jobs that indirectly make the work possible.

EDUCATION: NEW SCHOOL

Being a kid today is different than it's ever been before. Socially, the Internet has changed everything. A bully's power can turn monstrous in an irreversible instant with the amplifier of the Internet, and the pressure to cultivate and maintain an appealing online persona has intensified social pressures for all of us. Overcrowded classrooms and smartphones buzzing in backpacks are portals to distraction a thousand times more powerful than the old window to the playground. Many kids take ADHD drugs to lean against that avalanche of distraction, since we take it for granted that the curriculum isn't going to give them something to wake up for.

Education is our society's primary tool for upward mobility, and yet we have a bipolar schooling that verges on a caste system—one track for the rich, one for the poor, with very little opportunity to move up. The profound changes we're seeing all over our world don't often get represented in the curriculum, which can make kids feel alienated by the perceived pointlessness of what they're learning. Standardized testing in the United States has butted out arts education and treated the diverse needs of kids have with a uniform tablespoon of the same industrial syrup.

Getting into university consumes much of the focus of the second half of high school, and the advantage goes to candidates with money for private tutors, extracurricular trips abroad, and university visits. Even once you're in university, you might be accruing heaps and heaps of debt, learning about subjects that seem more arcane than ever, rightly uneasy about how these expensive 4 years are going to prepare you for a job.

And yet while the reality for schoolchildren, high school students, and university students has fundamentally transformed, the methods we use to organize and instruct them are a relic of simpler times. The concept of compulsory, classroom-based public education paid for by taxpayers arose during the Enlightenment. With the rise of factory jobs, western European economies needed an efficient process to train the next generation of workers. The problem is that as the world has shifted and the locus of jobs has moved from the factory into a diverse range of new industries, schools haven't. We need schools to catch up and prepare people for a different skill set, even a different way of thinking than they were designed to do.

The DC public school district is one of the worst in the United States. There's a great disparity in the dropout rates reported by DC and outside sources, but the number hovers somewhere between an abysmal 49 percent and an abysmal 63 percent. Only around 29 percent of public school graduates move on to secondary education.[8] When faced with a crisis of this magnitude, where does one begin? Tutoring? High school curriculum? More standardized tests? What about something that addresses a more deeply ingrained matter in students—their sense of their own possibilities?

When an attorney for the US Department of Justice visited

---

[8] Civic Enterprises. "The silent epidemic: perspectives of high school dropouts." 2006.

an Anacostia high school classroom in 1996 and asked students what would help them do better in school, they told him they needed jobs. Not better teachers, not a more compelling curriculum—jobs.

What was the connection between success in school and work? Perhaps the kids were speaking to their immediate needs, but they also revealed a deeper issue: Many students in these failing schools don't have adult role models employed in the professional sector, so for them, that world may as well exist on a distant, inaccessible planet. Many of these students look around them, at the endless unemployment, the crime, the poverty, and calculate their slim odds for launching a career. So what's the point of finishing high school?

The attorney was able to find internships for five of the Anacostia students, and out of that effort arose an organization he called Urban Alliance. Partnering with companies and organizations as diverse as law firms, government offices, and youth centers, the World Bank, and *National Geographic*, Urban Alliance offers enrolled students a kind of professional boot camp. During the school year, the students work paid afternoon internships at their assigned organization, under the wing of a volunteer mentor who gives them assignments and shows them the ropes at the company. On Fridays, the interns regroup at Urban Alliance headquarters for advice on practical information many kids never get: comportment in a business atmosphere, financial planning, applying for college, and resume-building. And there's time for homework too. Over the summer, the students have full-time internships and often develop professional relationships that last into their adult years.

The principle behind Urban Alliance's approach was simple: Provide students with the tools and confidence to enter the professional world, and you provide them with a reason to finish school. And it's working: Of the 1,100 students who have gone through the Urban Alliance program in the past 15 years, nearly 100 percent have graduated high school, and 88 percent have gone on to secondary education. A new branch of Urban Alliance is now launching in Baltimore. The Urban Alliance model shows us that it's okay to start small. Remember: In the beginning, there was only the problem of finding internships for five students.

Improving our education system has the potential to make a positive impact on so many deeply entrenched problems—health, personal finance, the creation of compassionate citizens of the world. Progress itself relies on an educated populace. Schooling should be a democratized path to hope, yet the outdated model of the classroom exacerbates as many problems as a healthy educational system might help solve: When schools fail, crime, poverty, and teen pregnancy proliferate.

The silver lining to the tangle of problems afflicting our educational system is that there are lots of nodes we can find to effect change. When a Silicon Valley hedge fund analyst named Sal Khan started using an online blackboard to do online tutoring for his cousins, he hardly knew he'd end up creating a free global teaching tool that delivers millions of lessons each month. Khan Academy has over 2,000 online videos—everything from a 2-minute arithmetic lesson to a 12-minute explanation of fractional reserve banking—and over 100 self-paced exercises. Sal still tries to upload five new lessons to the academy a day.

Innovations for Learning, a nonprofit whose mission is to

make educational technology affordable for K-12 classrooms, has developed a TeacherMate differentiated instruction system that allows students to work through lesson plans, educational games, exercises, and homework at their own pace. Variations of this basic program are popping up all over the world and bridging the gap in many places where teachers don't have effective or up-to-date curriculum or where they face classrooms of 50 or 100 students, making focused learning all but impossible. For younger generations, sometimes called digital natives, these new supercheap, handheld teaching tools can provide the interactive and fun content they've come to expect.

With dynamic lessons and interactive exercises available for free, and affordable devices that allow children to learn at their own pace, teachers are freed up to offer personalized help and to facilitate conversations and project-based learning opportunities that engage students and help them connect the classroom to real-world solutions. Increasingly, teachers are flipping the traditional model of classroom lesson plans and homework and projects at home. They can assign the video lesson plans for homework and use classroom time for conversations and special projects.

Many educational systems make it their goal to get every student college-ready, whether or not they have any interest (or use!) for college. For many students who have pressing needs at home or just can't connect the dots between algebra and the work they want or need to be doing, this is a source of frustration and a leading cause of dropping out. In Germany, students are given a choice between a vocational training in a career track of their choice or a general education college-prep track.

For those later in life who just want to learn about topics

that interest them or cultivate specific skills without applying to an educational program, do-it-yourself options abound. TED.com has over 1,000 of the most brilliant, inspiring, and educational presentations on topics from vulnerability to preserving seed varieties to ending polio forever. A new for-profit education start-up called Skillshare offers a way to connect individuals who want to teach a class to people who want to learn. Their motto is "learn anything from anyone." By connecting people with specific skills with people who want to learn, a whole new business model for education is born, with opportunities for teachers and learners alike.

THE ARTS: ENTERTAINMENT TOMORROW

Sitting together on a recent panel on the future of entertainment were four minds who seemed likely to know better than the rest of us about the coming possibilities for the arts: the founder of Twitter, one of the founders of Hulu, a vice president at MTV, and the CEO of Yahoo. They bantered about the democratization of content and the role recent technology has had in altering the business model that mainstream networks have relied on for decades. Watching the panel, noting the open-endedness of the conversation, the sense that no one knew what came next, Dev wrote in his notebook: *They are desperate for a new model of delivering entertainment, and they don't have the answers. Who is going to figure this out?*

Although these four people are captaining multi-billion-dollar ships through the turbulent waters of the entertainment industry, none of them knew what was ahead. The one thing they did agree on was that what might have worked yesterday wouldn't work tomorrow and that the future was up for grabs.

In the past 10 years, content has become available to us largely for free—access to movies, television, music, and writing has shifted to the open marketplace of the Internet. We're so used to enjoying our cultural content for free that it's becoming harder and harder to get us to pay for it.

The crumbling revenue model for the arts is echoed by a cascading collapse of many of the cultural institutions we took for granted as safe. Arts programs in schools are getting defunded; libraries, bookstores, newspapers, magazines, and museums are vanishing at an astonishing rate. Reality content and homemade videos rewire the appetites of the masses.

But overall, global demand for culture is stronger than ever. Aesthetics, stories, music, reflection, imagination that brilliantly transforms the facts of our reality—our desire for these things has never been greater. Though our traditional models for the funding, creation, and popularization of art are hitting a wall, we must see desire for culture and unprecedented ease with disseminating it as a doorway to new avenues of cultural growth.

NewspaperDeathWatch.com, a Web site that keeps a running tally of the closure of US metropolitan dailies, captures the overall picture neatly with its tagline: "Chronicling the Decline of Newspapers and the Rebirth of Journalism." News is thriving. There are over 125 million blogs at the time of this writing, with over a million new posts every day. Twitter sees 177 million tweets and Facebook 60 million status updates every single day. Even if the vast majority of these communications is empty content, the haul still represents an enormous increase in reporting what's going on in the world. And here's the rub: While the number of full-time paid journalists for big media companies is in decline, for roughly half a million Americans, blogging is their primary source of income. There are more paid bloggers than there are firefighters, CEOs, even computer programmers. Many make good salaries too: $45,000 to $90,000 a year but that doesn't mean we should all just become bloggers.[9]

The evolving business models in each sector of the arts—music, visual arts, literature, dance—are all different, but the basic pattern is the same. The Internet has created a distribution platform to reach more people than ever, but competition for eyeballs (or eardrums) is fierce and the old pay-for-content approach is a tough sell when there's so much free content to be had. So where does the money come from? For savvy marketers, the opportunities on the Internet to reach a niche audience is what pays the rent.

Billy's best friend growing up built a Web site for a friend of his parents on Long Island to sell Netsuke (pronounced Netsky), an obscure form of Japanese miniature sculpture. We never understood why, but the things flew off the (virtual) shelf. So while a Netsuke store in Long Island would have a hard time keeping the doors open with sales based on local foot traffic, they can reach virtually the entire global market for Netsuke with a Web site they paid a kid $500 to make.

Perry Chan is reinventing the arts by transforming the business model. Perry has worked in a range of careers over the years—everything from day trading to teaching at a preschool to running an art gallery in Brooklyn. Recognizing the need, he started a company called Kickstarter in 2009 that helps people with artistic projects raise money from friends, family, and the

[9] Penn, Mark, and E. Kinney Zalesene. "America's Newest Profession: Bloggers for Hire" Wall Street Journal 21 Apr. 2009.

broader Kickstarter community. Kickstarter is democratizing the patron/artist relationship and enabling anyone to play either of the traditionally guarded roles. The artists determine what rewards they offer for different funding levels, upload a compelling video, and begin canvassing for cash, and patrons can browse stories and rewards and play rainmaker to any number of ideas. In the first two years, over $60 million has been raised on the platform by nearly 10,000 projects.

Some of you may be wondering how the arts slipped into this chapter on major sectors of the economy that hold promise for recovery and rebuilding. By revealing or reflecting on injustice, corruption, and suffering, by elevating the stories of those who too often pass under the radar, visual artists, writers, and musicians have always been able to help create and inspire progress in our world. While the sector employs at least 6 million Americans, it's also a critical part of the broader transformation. Jeff Chang, author of *Can't Stop, Won't Stop: A History of the Hip Hop Generation*, argued in *The Nation* for "A Creativity Stimulus" as part of a broader national recovery plan:

> "Every moment of major social change requires a collective leap of imagination. Political transformation must be accompanied not just by spontaneous and organized expressions of unrest and risk but by an explosion of mass creativity . . . Creativity can be a powerful form of organizing communities from the bottom up. The economic crisis gives us a chance to rethink the role of creativity in making a vibrant economy and civil society. Artists as well as community organizers cultivate new forms of knowledge and

consciousness. One of the unsung stories of the past 25 years is how both have used creativity to inspire community development and renewal. Creativity has become the glue of social cohesion in times of turmoil."

We need the magnetism and liberating imagination of artists to popularize and organize our movement. As powerful new poles in the art world emerge, places like Shanghai and Mexico City, young creatives give new expressions and cultural resonance to efforts for change. But there are also plenty of opportunities for artists to apply their talents to projects with transformative impact, from mural arts initiatives, to music showcases to benefit charity, to grassroots transformation of urban spaces, to inner-city tutoring programs.

It's an uphill battle for the arts, as it always has been. But the readers, the watchers, and the listeners are there, waiting for something brilliant and new, something that shows our world from a previously unseen angle. And where there's an audience, there's an opportunity for a show.

HEALTH: HEALERS AND THE GLOBAL HEALTH REVOLUTION

Billy
When Wahleah was pregnant with our first little girl, we spent a lot of time talking about where she would labor and give birth. Wahleah was drawn to traditional methods still in use by many of her people. For my part, I was conflicted between my worried mom and sister, who wanted us to use a hospital, and the books and articles I had read about the loss of control of the

childbirth process, skyrocketing rates of C-sections, and other awful-sounding aspects of hospital births. We found a group of amazing midwives, several of whom had delivered thousands of healthy babies at home, and began going together for Wahleah's checkups. And we also registered at the hospital, just in case.

We were at home on a cold and sunny February morning when Wahleah felt the first contraction. She was smiling when she came upstairs to my office and quietly told me. Labor was sporadic and slow to start, and we spent most of the day walking around the house, gently bouncing on the big red ball. I set up an inflatable bathtub in my office, which was just next door to our bedroom, where we'd planned to have the delivery. Her water broke around 8 p.m. I was glad to have the midwives, but especially Wahleah's sister, Elisha, a one-time WNBA prospect, girls' basketball coach, and mother of four, whose expertise with labor was supplemented by some privileged understanding of her sister's idiosyncrasies. The 12 hours of active labor remain the most heroic thing I've ever seen, and at the end, Wahleah, relieved, exhausted, finally delivered our first daughter. At my father-in-law's suggestion, we named her Tohaana, Guardian of Water in Navajo.

Wahleah's mom put corn pollen in our little one's quivering mouth. Her dad sang to her and pointed the crown of her head toward our fireplace to allow the spirits in the fire to seal the soft top of her head. My mom and sister rocked her with delight. We were all crying and laughing, taking turns holding this perfect bundled beauty. I couldn't believe how little and light she was, her dark shock of silk glimmering in the firelight.

We brought her upstairs for Sierra, one of the midwives, to run the Apgar test a second time to check her vitals. Sierra looked worried. Her scores were lower, she was having trouble breathing. The car was already loaded with the new car seat we had gotten a few weeks prior, so Sierra, Tohaana, my mom, and I packed in quickly and drove to the hospital.

By the time we got there, her skin was a pale blue color. We rushed to the pediatric center, got a respirator on the baby, and a young doctor named Ron Tuckman quickly checked her and said, "I know you wanted a very hands-off, natural birth, but this is now going to have to be very hands-on." He took us over to the neonatal center for more tests. They poked and pricked and taped on sensors that fed the constantly beeping machines, whose rhythms and alarms are forever burned into Wahleah's and my head. We came to think of the nurses as angels—so many brought a love and good attention that these troubled infants, many without parents visiting often if at all, needed so badly.

After 8 days, we were able to take our little warrior home. She needed to be kept on a respirator, but we were home. Wahleah's parents made her a cradle board, and Tohaana slept. Bundled in blankets, her 7- and 8-hour naps and good nighttime sleeps had us constantly peeking, checking for the regular rise and fall of her little chest. She could breathe. We could breathe.

And then came the bill: $40,978—an almost incomprehensible sum. I had insurance for both Wahleah and myself and had added Tohaana a day after she was born, but the insurance company said we hadn't properly registered Tohaana at the hospital and wouldn't pay. A year and countless hours trying to get my insurance company and the hospital to stop blaming each other and just work it out, the bills kept coming and bill collectors kept hassling us. Just after I successfully got my insurance to pay up and call the dogs off, a new bill came from the hospital—this time for $7,188—to cover some additional costs of her first few days there that insurance declined to cover. By now, I was a pro. This one only took a couple months to shake off.

Dev

My grandparents live in a rural town of 3,000 called Lake Cowichan, on Vancouver Island. It's a nice place to visit, but not the best place to fall ill. One morning in the spring of 2011, my grandfather felt faint, had to sit down, and called my grandmother over. He thought he was having a heart attack. My grandmother gave him an aspirin and called 911.

Within 20 minutes, the ambulance was there and my grandfather was on the way to the mini hospital in a small town 35 minutes away. They took him in right away, assessed his case, gave him a temporary treatment to ensure he was stable, and sent him to waiting doctors at the major hospital in Victoria to perform the emergency angioplasty.

The doctors, the hospital, and my grandmother did it all right, it ran smoothly, and by the time I got the phone call from my mother, about 6 hours after my grandfather had felt faint, the situation was under control and my parents were relaxed. My grandfather was in recovery, and doctors had confirmed that he had no permanent heart damage.

The cost here in Canada for that kind of service: zero.

You don't even realize it, as a Canadian, until you start to have close American friends and begin to hear their stories. I remember being totally shocked when Billy told me he was paying over $1,400 a month on health insurance for his family. At the time, it was as much as I was paying for rent.

Our system isn't perfect by any means. It is under constant debate and criticism—a lack of doctors, underfunded preventive health, agonizing wait times for elective surgeries, and the constant push to move to some sort of public/private hybrid, but all that being said, no one worries about getting sick for financial reasons.

Still, regardless of the differences between the American and Canadian systems, there is one thing you can be sure of: There is a lot of opportunity to reinvent and rethink our approach to healthcare. Study after study shows that preventive care is the most cost-efficient kind of health intervention. If people were serious about cutting costs in the system, low-cost programs in communities to ensure good health through better diet and exercise and to provide regular checkups to spot problems before they get bad is where it's at. The relative focus on patching up disasters rather than preventing them remains a problem in most healthcare programs around the world.

As this problem is fixed, huge opportunities will open up to a wave of healers in community clinics, health clubs, community centers, and hospitals. Entrepreneurial answers that have the potential to reshape healthcare are being supported by incubators like Rock Health, which is seeking to empower its members to use the technological creativity found in social media and games and focus it on rethinking healthcare.

We don't always need hundred-thousand-dollar machines to create life-changing fixes. With a nonprofit called Embrace, Jane Chen and Rahul Panicker have designed a $25 incubator and aim to save 135,000 babies in India after 5 years and reduce the health problems of another 3.8 million. The cost to fix the common problem of blinding cataracts was $300 for intraocular lenses and largely out of reach of most people in the world. A simple surgery replaced the clouded lens with a plastic lens, and a single doctor could cure more than 100 people a day.

In Tamil Nadu, a southernmost part of India, a retired eye doctor called Dr. V, who had performed cataract surgeries for over 20 years, was forced into mandatory retirement. Seeing the problem he'd worked so hard to solve only getting worse, he started a small local clinic that he has grown into a network of Aravind Eye Hospitals, one of the largest providers of eye care in the world. Instead of focusing on extracting the highest possible profit from each operation performed, which drives medical innovation in many companies to this day, Dr. V built an alternative model of healthcare that provided low-cost and free care to poor people without other options. The only thing limiting the number of surgeries was the steep cost of the lenses.

In the early 1990s, David Green, who worked with the Seva Foundation on eliminating curable blindness, suggested to Dr. V that Seva and Aravind partner on a factory to produce the lenses more cheaply. They raised the money and were able to cut the costs to $10 or less a pair. The combination of Aravind's innovative care system and radically cheaper technology now allows Aravind to treat 1.7 million people a year (two-thirds for free) and the factory to produce 10 percent of the global intraocular lens market. After seeing the incredible benefit that cheaper medical technologies could bring to millions of people, Green turned to sterile surgical sutures and then hearing aids. Since his products are made to high standards, and usually cost only 5 to 20 percent of the price to produce, he now sells them in over 100 countries.

One of the biggest long-term opportunities for health will come from health records around the world going online.

It will save patients the incredibly stupid chore of filling out health information each visit, and it will save nurses and doctors an enormous amount of time transferring notes from one paper format to another. But most important, it is the foundation of a global health data set that can be used to crack the code on countless chronic diseases and to roll out digital diagnostic programs online at home and in community health centers that are more affordable, accessible, and accurate for most ailments, reducing the stress on health systems across the world. No need for time-consuming on-off research projects. We could soon have a billion health records powering researchers in the lab and healers on the frontlines of a global health revolution.

FOOD: A DIABLO BURGER (AND FRIES)

Food doesn't need to be reinvented; our problem is that we do too much of that already. We're ingesting chemistry sets full of things we'd never consume on their own in the name of better taste and a smaller gut. We're introducing frog genes into our cherry tomatoes to make them more drought resistant, and we're planting seeds altered to withstand high doses of pesticides. We've forgotten what grandmothers around the world have long told us: You are what you eat.

For thousands of years, people have adapted to a variety of traditional diets based on understanding about health and longevity, the availability of local produce, peer-tested recipes, elder knowledge passed down from generation to generation in a history of responses to a simple question: What should we eat tonight? These traditions have produced what we recognize as the Mediterranean, the Indian, the Japanese, and Middle Eastern diets, diets that we are just now "proving" lead to long lives with little chronic illness. The other conclusion that science has made strikingly clear is that the diet worst for us is also the fastest-growing diet in the world: the modern Western diet.

Hamburgers and fries, microwavable pastry-shelled fat bombs we eat on the go, unconsciously, and platters of meat and cheese with a side of hash browns and gravy, all washed down with a Diet Coke. It's no wonder that our rates for diabetes, heart disease, cancer, and obesity are so out of control.

The story of our industrial food system and modern Western diet is one of astounding technological innovation. After World War II, the so-called "Green Revolution" changed agriculture around the world, bringing pesticide, fertilizer, intensive irrigation, and high-yielding varieties of crops to farmers. These techniques have allowed agricultural production to keep pace with the explosion in population growth, saving hundreds of millions of lives, but their emphasis on scale of production left behind a toxic legacy, eroded topsoil, and pushed water tables to dangerously low levels, as well as disrupted food markets and forced small farmers to abandon generations of sustainable food production to seek jobs in urban areas.

With the consensus on good nutrition and sustainable land use growing ever more clear, and with the growing public fascination with food origins and the culinary arts, there's a bounty of opportunity for people who want to get involved in participating in the new alternative. There's a little burger joint in Flagstaff, Arizona, called Diablo Burger, co-owned by Eli and Derrick, which is doing just that. Billy and Dev went there first thing on Dev's first visit to Flagstaff. They grabbed beers and stools, and as they waited for their burgers, Dev flipped over the menu, where there is written a poem entitled *Terroir-ist Manifesto* for eating in place.

The power of that word *Terroir* resonated with Dev. It connoted an idea that location matters, that we can sense our connection to the soil and all the processes that go into the food on our plate by noticing how our food captures its tastes. This burger was made from lean grass fed beef produced by the Diablo Land Trust, just east of Flagstaff, and everything else on this plate was either from a local purveyor or from a small, local business. And this burger tasted especially good. A couple of days later, Billy and Dev sat down with Eli to talk to him about how the manifesto ended up on the back of the menu and what exactly was going on with his burger.

Eli put in our order for a vitamin B burger—beet, bacon, and goat cheese on a burger stuffed between slices of an English muffin branded with the letters DB—and led us out to the back patio. Eli had grown up in Santa Cruz, went on to study conservation biology at UC Santa Cruz, and became another version of everyone we had been talking to: adrift, then an activist, then an academic, always asking the big questions on how all of his experience fit together.

He decided to take a risk after undergrad on the UCSC Farm and Garden program on a two-month apprenticeship in small-scale food production. Working with his hands, he uncovered a disconnect. "My interests weren't reflective of the way things were studied or even communicated. There was a gap between conservation biology and the people growing food and thinking about food production. I wanted to bridge that gap—to be able to make the connection that no one was making."

So after the two months, Eli registered for a graduate program at Northern Arizona University. There he reengaged with a
new program that educated low-income communities about the
connection between sustainable food and conservation. He got
his degree and entered The Wilderness, wondering what to do
with his passions, his abilities, the broken policies, the people he
knew. This Wilderness was worsened by the isolating frustrations
of the recession. "I just saw the constraints within academia and
the constraints within the government sector to do radical, progressive things on the ground." He felt stuck. But one day, he was
playing tennis with Derrick, a friend from the conservation world,
who asked him between sets, "What about a burger shop?"

Eli instantly saw the possibilities beyond opening up a new
place to eat. "Here is an opportunity to have people across the
board come in and enjoy delicious food and just by enjoying that
food create positive conservation benefits, and it didn't matter if I
convinced them if they needed to do it or not. They were having a
great meal and that was convincing enough. I started to think
about the old environmental approach of 'let me show you how
big my stick is' so you will do what I want you to do or you will be
deemed a bad person—that's done." Now, Eli told us, we have to
take the approach, "How can I get you passionately involved,
excited, and profitable, whether it is profit through your own
health or creating a business? How can I demonstrate that doing
the right thing is fun and can make you money?"

Eli had been asking the same question as everyone else,
except he had found his answer: He was a conservation biolo-
gist who found his calling as a burger man. We don't all have to
start flipping burgers to seize the thousands of ways to find

our place within the rediscovery and rebuilding of how we eat food, how we nourish and sustain ourselves. Farm to table, and everything in between.

Healthy fast food is actually an important part of the solution. Nate Appleman is a well-known San Francisco–based chef, and after seeing through the launch of Pulino's in New York—driving a local and organic food agenda—he quit. He is now working for Chipotle Mexican Grill, the fast food burrito maker. At first the food blogs were taken aback with headlines like *WTF? Post Pulino's, Nate Appleman Lands a Job at Chipotle*, but it was in one of these interviews where he explained his goal: "What led me to this was being able to make a change. I was just trying to figure out, 'How can I make a difference?' It's one thing to be a really good chef and cook, and it's another to impact millions of people—from the farmers, ranchers, and everyone down to the 20,000 employees. As you get older and wiser, you're looking for more fulfillment."

Bryant Terry is another friend who found his life's work in reinventing the way we eat and relate to our food. His latest cookbook is called *Vegan Soul Kitchen*, and it takes on the task of reinventing the African-American food culture in a way that is healthy, vegetarian, and sustainable. One meal and one recipe at a time, Bryant's strategy is about showing people that eating healthy doesn't have to mean eating bland.

There are opportunities to reinvent the way we consume, think about, and relate to the food we eat all around us. What's your role in recreating our food system? Are you mainly just a conscious eater and occasional cook? Or would you enjoy getting your hands a little dirty, planting a backyard or kitchen garden, or helping friends grow on a bigger plot? Maybe you know of some empty lots in the suburbs that you can imagine transforming into small, community-supported farms? Maybe you can ask some neighbors to let you pick their fruit, redistributing the surplus to friends or a food bank, convince a local restaurant to transition to produce grown by local farmers, or even earn a couple hundred bucks a week selling breakfast sandwiches at a nearby farmers' market?

STUFF: RISE OF THE LANDFILL EATERS

In 2009, Nikhil Arora was about to turn his new degree from UC Berkeley's Haas School of Business into a consulting career, and Alejandro Velez was getting ready to move out of his frat house to take an offer from a New York investment bank. But in 6 months, both of them would be standing knee deep in coffee grounds in a small Berkeley warehouse and would be known to clients as the Mushroom Guys.

It was their business ethics professor who planted the first seed of that unlikely path, when he used an example in class about how coffee grounds were *the* model of inefficiency—a single cup of coffee from many beans, used once—and how they could actually be used to grow organics. After the class, both Alex and Nikhil approached the professor to learn more, and the professor suggested the students go after answers together.

Two weeks later, Nikhil and Alex hit up the local hardware store and Starbucks, and picked up 10 paint buckets and a bunch of free coffee grounds. They planted some mushrooms and tucked them all away in a closet at the fraternity house, and a few weeks later, Nikhil awoke to a call from Alex. He was back from spring break and had opened the door to the closet in his frat house to find 9 out of 10 buckets "fruiting." One bucket had a full array of perfectly formed mushrooms.

Not having the expertise to distinguish a good mushroom from a dud, and with a little daring and their best bucket from the closet, they headed to Chez Panisse, Alice Water's iconic restaurant in Berkeley's Gourmet Ghetto, a pioneer in the local and organic food movement. Waters happened to be there, heard the boys' story, and gamely inspected their haul. Her executive chef fried them up, and Waters liked what she tasted. Within a few weeks, Alex and Nikhil were heading up an e-mail chain leading directly to the buyer for northern California Whole Foods, who agreed to carry their crop.

Four months later, Alex and Nikhil had not only figured out how to grow mushrooms, but they had also determined how to get paid for every part of the process. They got paid by the coffee shop as a "waste management expert" to pick up the coffee grounds, they grew and sold the mushrooms to Whole Foods, and they then turned around and packaged the resulting compost, selling it to local gardening stores. It's what sustainability experts call a "closed loop." Today, Alex and Nikhil's company, BTTR Ventures (for Back to the Roots), sells their grow-your-own mushroom kits at Whole Foods nationwide and is on pace to collect, divert, and reuse 1 million pounds of coffee grounds this year. Their company has inspired dozens of similar companies in Mexico City, Madrid, London, Delhi, and around the world.

Our counters and closets and garages and storage lockers are just brief detours on our stuff's eventual passage to the garbage pile. Almost everything you see around you is future trash. In our current throwaway economy, many products are actually designed for the dump. Some companies that make money selling people stuff would prefer those people threw out the stuff they bought or that is broken, so they can sell some more stuff.

Stuff isn't going away, no matter how critical we become of it: Our desire to give things to people we love, our desire for little comforts and luxuries, our desire to participate in the culture by following trends, our desire for hobbies and treasures and collections that make us feel unique—it expresses our personality to others. We all know that even as some of us learn to live with less, others around the world are learning to live with more. The key is figuring out a way to prevent all that stuff from becoming *waste*.

While most people are familiar with the concept of recycling, there are actually two kinds of recycling: upcycling and downcycling. Most recycling today is downcycling. When we separate our cans from our newspaper from our shrink wrap, those materials are grouped with like items and mixed together or melted to produce lower-grade plastic or paper pulp. Office paper becomes cardboard. Water bottles become speed bumps. Nikhil and Alex are upcycling—converting waste into products of higher value and environmental benefit.

These landfill eaters are cropping up all over the place in all different forms. Kosaka Smelting and Refining Company in Japan heats up old electronics to 1,300 degrees and is able to recover 19 different metals—pretty critical when many of these metals (used in all different kinds of computing and clean energy technologies) are growing scarce. The Rebuilders Source in New York City's South Bronx neighborhood salvages building materials from construction and demolition sites, cleans them up, and resells them to contractors and regular folks in the community. Like TerraCycle in the US, Darpana, Thunk, and Green the Gap all upcycle plastic bags and weave them into bags, wallets, and purses. Conserve India, founded by two fashion technology graduates, has developed a technology to compress newspaper and plastic and make a material with the texture of leather, from which they make clothes, bags, and shoes.

One of the things Nikhil told us really stuck: The exciting lesson from BTTR's success is that we produce so much trash and in such concentrated amounts that if you can think of one thing, one item in your daily life—straws, pens, computers, old clothes, or even coffee grounds—you can build a business model that involves collecting, repurposing, and selling it.

Look around you. Take a quick mental catalog of 15 to 20 things in the room, plane, or wherever you're sitting right now. What materials are those things made from? How can you imagine some of those materials being repurposed? If you were able to collect tens of thousands of that item for free—or, maybe even get paid to collect them from people—what could you do with them?

Maybe you make roof insulation with old pillows and jeans, or collect and resell old tires to builders of eco-houses like earthships. What could be done with the huge trash bags full of leaves and pine needles that line the sidewalks across the country each fall? There is gold stuffed in our closets and drawers, left on curbs, and in mountains of trash and alleyway dumpsters all over the country. We have only to find it, use the power of our imagination to clean it off, and give it new life.

DID WE MISS YOUR INDUSTRY?

We've given you seven examples of industries that are shifting and evolving today, some in ways that will constitute massive transformation. They are being rebuilt by entrepreneurs and the people who support them. They are being built by people with real jobs, making real money and a fundamental difference in how our world operates.

So how do you stake out a job for yourself in an industry that we haven't talked about in this book? We're going to give you some steps to rethink the possibilities for any industry, steps you can follow to find a job or to become the next entrepreneur shaping an industry today. There are four questions to ask yourself to begin uncovering the opportunities and the potential leaders to work with in your particular industry. The questions below are meant just to spark some thoughts and give you a starting line for your explorations into reinventing whatever industry that you are a part of.

1. WHY DOES THE INDUSTRY EXIST?
Why does this industry exist? What fundamental need does it meet? Does it make sure people can travel great distances quickly, or does it answer the question of how we find out about the world around us? How will the needs look different if you zoomed out 10, 20, or even 50 years? Express your answer to this question in the form of a human need that will be around for many years to come.

2. WHAT'S BROKEN?
Asking what is broken about the current system can be a powerful yet daunting task. Sometimes the answer is found only in conversations with people who have been in the industry for years, and other times, what's broken is commonly understood by almost everyone. Knowing the current limitations,

flaws, and challenges can help you identify gaps that you can fill and opportunities for innovation. How could you meet the industry's function better and make it more sustainable and more efficient? Where are the opportunities for reinvention?

3. WHAT ARE THE MAVERICKS DOING?

Once you begin to look, you will find people who are already working on these core questions, rethinking industries from the ground up. This is one of your greatest assets today. They may be answering the question in a different way than you envision answering it, but like you, they are just beginning to figure it out—improvising, experimenting, piloting new untested methods, and answering similar questions.

Although some of them may seem intimidatingly far along, in reality, most understand that as pioneers they need fresh people to collaborate with. These will be your peers, collaborators, board members, and potential bosses. Get to know what they are doing, what questions they are asking, and how they have found funding that allowed them to dedicate themselves fully to realizing their answer to that core question.

4. WHO ARE THE WINNERS?

Understanding who profits as a result of your industry's improved redesign will help you immediately recognize who will fund your work, who will hire you, or who will eventually acquire the company you start. Who currently "wins" as a result of this industry being fixed? You can guarantee that the companies already firmly entrenched in answering this question are looking for the ways to recreate and rebuild in response to our changing environment. What you can uniquely offer them is the flexibility, the creativity, and the low stakes often needed to take a gamble on something new.

The people who stand to profit from your redesign are the people to look to in order to pay your bills, to invest in your company, or to kick-start your career. If you can help an established company see the long-term benefits of being out ahead and shifting gears to be part of the noble solution, the decision makers will want to support you. The real solutions are almost always good for multiple parties, and these types of solutions are going to come from people like you, who can solve intractable problems with fresh eyes.

DAILY PRACTICE #3: ENOUGH

STEP 1: SEE YOURSELF

I am not educated enough. I am not smart enough. I don't have enough time. I don't have enough energy. I'm too broke. I can't even find a job to hold down. I've never had a bolt-of-lightning epiphany. I don't have what it takes to rebuild an entire industry. I am not enough . . .

When friends tell you they're not good enough for something they want, it's very easy to confront their attitude as insecurity or a cop-out. But why is it so hard to see our own feelings of insufficiency as mental blocks?

You can tell yourself every morning in the mirror, *I am the best.* But believing you're enough and behaving like it too takes more than just daily affirmation. How can you remind yourself you're enough when you feel like crap, when you have a bad day, or when you get rejected? This practice is about understanding that it's natural and important to feel bad sometimes, that you don't have to "positive think" your way out of it, but you should know you have everything you need to brush yourself off and continue with your life.

Integrating this practice into your life will provide you with a sustaining foundation of confidence you need to take on an entire industry, to find jobs where others can't, and to build a career making good.

We live in a time where marketers and cultural narratives are constantly reinforcing the message that we aren't enough— that we don't have enough time, money, attractiveness, or intelligence. When we look at life through the lens of "it's not enough," we find evidence everywhere we look. This "evidence" is not hard to find if we're seeking it. Our emotions, our nervous system follow and respond. We operate from fear. We feel contracted, hypervigilant, as we engage in a relentless battle with a world in which there's never enough.

But there is another possible perspective: There is enough.

When we look at life through this second lens, "there is enough," we can also find plenty of supporting evidence. As we look and start to see sufficiency, we begin to operate more from trust. We feel more at ease. We are more willing to take appropriate risks. We begin to see opportunities and find allies that were not apparent when operating from self-defeating scarcity.

"Not enough" and "enough" are different lenses on reality. Life is vast and incomprehensible. To make sense of reality, we screen or filter out most of what's out there. Our perceptual filters are not neutral. We sort and screen according to our beliefs. We make up stories about how life is—*it's this way, it's that way. I'm this type of person, I'm that type of person.*

The habitual stories we tell ourselves have tremendous

impact on our experience. These stories are, to a large degree, the product of our life experience and our conditioning—personal, cultural, or relating to our social identity. Some of these perspectives are inherently empowering, building us up, helping us achieve our dreams and vision. Other stories are disempowering, taking away our motivation and energy, limiting our effectiveness and feelings of fulfillment.

It is important to know that these stories are not objective translations of reality. We developed them in response to our early environments. Many are echoes of the stories our parents told us. They evolve in response to being measured against society's dominant values of success. Some are internalized notions about our race, gender, culture, or sexual orientation.

We live in a world that constantly reaffirms to us that we aren't enough, so don't judge yourself for encountering these feelings. The simple act of noticing empowers you to take control in moments of insecurity. In each moment of doubt, you can simply leverage gratitude for what you have and pride in what you've done to flip your lens and see that you are already *enough*.

And yet, we all still struggle with "not enough." More of our struggle is with our own psychology. We struggle with the impact of our own life experiences. We struggle with our sense of self. We struggle with unequal treatment by the structures of society. We struggle with our own habits of mind and patterns of emotional responses.

Maybe life isn't exactly the way we want it, but is it sufficient? Perhaps it's sufficient enough that we might consider allowing ourselves to derive satisfaction and confidence from the many blessings of our life.

Observe each and every time your mind has the perception

or experience of scarcity, that there's not enough, or that you're not enough.

STEP 2: CELEBRATE SUFFICIENCY[10]

Find every opportunity you can to affirm sufficiency in your life. Acknowledge and celebrate your life, those around you, and yourself. See how many opportunities you can find to acknowledge and be grateful for:

* The support and love you receive from others

* How many people there are who care about making a better world

* The commitment and contributions of those you work with

* Your own commitment and contributions

* The food you eat each day that sustains you

* The comfort of your home and the relative abundance of your lifestyle

* The kindness and generosity of others

* The good ways in which you show up for others

* Everything positive in your life

Getting a blank piece of paper and just writing a list is a good place to start.

[10] This practice was inspired by Lynne Twist's wonderful book *The Soul of Money.*

THE SIX STEPS

CHAPTER 4

REFLECT

*"You have been telling the people that this is the
Eleventh Hour. Now you must go back and tell the
people that this is The Hour. And there are things to be
considered:*
Where are you living?
What are you doing?
What are your relationships?
Are you in right relation?
Where is your water?
Know your garden. It is time to speak your Truth.
*Create your community. Be good to each other. And do
not look outside yourself for the leader."*
—THE ELDERS ORAIBI, HOPI NATION
JUNE 8, 2000

Between the apocalyptic scenarios depicted in Hollywood movies, New Age forecasts for mass spiritual and cultural transformation, the conflicting accounts in Mayan history around 2012, and our perpetual high anxiety swirling around the next elections as if it'll be our last, there's a potent air of expectation around this moment in time.

All of the controversy and anxiety is indicative of how we understand transformation. We think about it arriving from the outside, descending upon us in a big event, apart from human agency. But it can be a long wait for a single moment of massive change, and societies don't revise themselves entirely on election night. External events can help catalyze or reinforce change, but what we're actually seeing right now is a ground-up, people-led shift, over time and in increments, based on the efforts and ideas of hundreds of millions of people.

Real change requires diligent mental and physical training and consistent effort. It's a marathon. It can be hard to imagine yourself stepping in to that kind of a commitment. We all have routines and patterns etched deeply into our lives, and finding free reign to start something ambitious might not be as appealing as the idea that change will arrive in a miracle moment. We just wish it were that simple. But let's get real.

Now we begin our training—preparing ourselves for real change in our own lives. This is about having the courage to ask ourselves tough questions, answer them honestly, and let the results direct changes in our lives. To really make good, we have to let go of some of our old assumptions and habits, many of which deliver us comforts and satisfactions we don't want to give up.

But letting go is exactly what we need to do today. If we don't rethink the way we do things now, we'll eat, burn, and waste everything of value on this planet.

In this chapter, we'll focus on three questions that will be a touchstone for the rest of the book, questions you will likely come back to again and again over the course of your life.

* How will I make money?

* What does doing good mean to me?

* How do I want to spend my time?

Big, intimidating questions, but in order to build the life we want, we need to seek their answers. For each, we'll look at how the habits and routines we've grown used to are stopping us from growing into our best selves, and we'll talk about some strategies to really get our personal house in order in preparation for the great work we need to do. The key to this chapter is to actually pause to reflect on the questions we pose.

This chapter isn't just about making yourself a good job candidate or even about getting yourself motivated to change the world. It's about fully rising to your own potential. At a 2011 Rockwood Fellows meeting, at which 35 of the most powerful social change leaders joined together to learn, share, and build, Billy was struck by the unvarnished truth in something social justice activist Adrienne Maree Brown said: "Action expresses priorities." Action comes down to how we behave and make choices on both the macro and micro levels—how we define our moral center, how we manage our time, and how we deal with money.

HOW WILL YOU MAKE MONEY?

Dev was in West Virginia with 25 other young people from around the world, and they were going around the circle talking about why everyone did the work that they did. A woman named Coumba, who writes and publishes children's books in West Africa, shared a short parable that spoke to her choices. It was a story about an American tourist and a Mexican fisherman. I now know it has been told for ages, with variations tracing as far back as 4th-century BC Chinese philosopher Chuang Tzu. It goes like this:

An American tourist was at the pier of a small coastal Mexican village when a small boat with just one fisherman docked.

Inside the small boat were several large yellowfin tuna. The tourist complimented the Mexican on the quality of his fish and asked how long it took to catch them.

The Mexican replied, "Only a little while."

The tourist then asked, "Why didn't you stay out longer and catch more fish?"

The Mexican said, "With this I have more than enough to support my family's needs."

The tourist then asked, "But what do you do with the rest of your time?"

The Mexican fisherman said, "I sleep late, fish a little, play with my children, take siesta with my wife, stroll into the village each evening where I sip wine and play guitar with my amigos. I have a full and busy life."

The tourist scoffed, "I can help you. You should spend more time fishing, and with the proceeds, buy a bigger boat. With the proceeds from the bigger boat, you could buy several boats. Eventually you would have a fleet of fishing boats. Instead of selling your catch to a middleman, you would sell directly to the processor, eventually opening your own cannery. You would control the product, processing, and distribution. You could leave this small coastal fishing village and move to Mexico City, then Los Angeles, and eventually New York, where you could run your ever-expanding enterprise."

The Mexican fisherman asked, "But, how long will this all take?"

The tourist replied, "15 to 20 years."

"But what then?" asked the Mexican.

The tourist laughed and said, "That's the best part. When the time is right, you would sell your company stock to the public and become very rich. You would make millions."

"Millions? . . . Then what?"

The American said, "Then you would retire, move to a small coastal fishing village where you would sleep late, fish a little, play with your kids, take siesta with your wife, stroll to the village in the evenings where you could sip wine and play your guitar with your amigos."

The realities of debt, bills, obligations, and the simple desire to participate in mainstream society prevent most of us from even considering going back to basics. The fundamental need to earn an income is the decisive factor for most people in what life path they take. In over a decade working with thousands of young people, we've come to see it as the biggest barrier to people following their passions and working to build a better world.

We also know that the glamorization of the poor is a fiction—that poverty correlates with stress, health problems, divorce, lack of education, and a short life span, and when it affects an entire culture, it can lead to worse: famine, war, and disease.

But there is some essential truth in this parable about the logical flaws in our culture's idealized goals, and there's evidence that suggests once we have enough money to comfortably cover a middle-class lifestyle, more money has absolutely no effect on our happiness. In the pursuit of money that affords us a lifestyle in which our needs are taken care of, oddly we lose track of what we want and what we most deeply care about. More "needs" creep in.

Lynne Twist wrote a beautiful book called *The Soul of Money,* which "is about our own soul and how and why we often eclipse it, dismiss it, or compromise it in our relationship with money: the way we get money, use money, give money, and sometimes just try to avoid thinking about money." A closer look at many of the most entrenched problems we face will more often than not take you back to an unrelenting greed that's baked into the economic models that dominate policy decisions around the world.

As long as Shell can profitably extract and sell oil from the Niger Delta, even if it means poisoning the people, fouling the whole region for generations, and propping up a vicious dictatorship that murders people who question the arrangement, it will continue to do so. When the community simply tried to end natural gas flaring, a practice of burning the gas released by oil drilling that covers the landscape with a toxic layer of soot, Shell would always come back saying it had a "fiduciary duty" to its shareholders and that stopping the practice was simply too costly. Its shareholders require a good return on their investment, and if they don't get it, they'll sell their shares and the company will lose value.

Though not so dramatic, the same basic dilemma takes place in dorm rooms and over dinner tables across the world. We ask ourselves and our spouses and friends, What choice do I have? We go to work each day to pay for the ever-increasing costs of life in the modern world, pay our rent, feed ourselves and our families, fill our car with gas, go on a date, or decompress at the movies.

On the Navajo reservation, where the people consider the deep seams of coal to be the liver of the sacred female mountains of Black Mesa, coal miners are the best-paid workers in the whole region, often supporting their whole extended family with their paycheck. As Anishinaabe activist and two-time US Green Party vice presidential candidate Winona LaDuke says, "We need to create a way of life where a community is not forced to cannibalize their mother in order to live."

How will you make the money you need to live well?

The most fundamental premise of this book is that you don't have to compromise your values to have comfort and control over your time. We are not saying it's easy or that you'll never have to bus tables or work odd jobs to make ends meet. We've spent 3 years digging into the barriers people are facing, uncovering the lessons from people who have made it work, and compiling tools and resources precisely because it hasn't been easy for many people. But in the process, we've also met so many people who have found that sweet spot, where making money and doing good overlap, that we know it's possible.

In the long term, we want to grow that overlap by incorporating our values into the economy. This change begins with our own choice to commit to a path that doesn't hurt people or the planet. It's a courageous choice, yes, but it's also a contagious choice—as more and more people see it's possible, they will want it for themselves, demand it of their companies and their governments. With good regulation, better incentives, a better values-based business culture, and more good people making waves in business, we'll bring the two circles into closer and closer alignment.

But just as important as paying attention to what you earn is watching what you spend. Many of us never got the basics of personal finance, but there are actually two sides to any budget: income and expenses. Ideally they match, or income is a little higher than expenses so you can have room for savings. When expenses run higher than income, the difference is debt. Debt is the killer, the curse, the plague.

Young people are targeted by credit card companies, seduced by promised benefits of a college degree, and encouraged to take on massive amounts of debt at a young age. You'll have the rest of your life to deal with it, they're told, a devil's bargain that often comes too true. The enormous debt burdens people carry distort their choices, crowding out passions, deferring dreams. Generation Debt, we've come to be called, tens of millions of young people taking loans from big banks to buy things they don't need or to get a diploma.

Former President Bill Clinton has recently joined a chorus of reformers, pointing out that in the United States, "In one decade, we went from 1st to 10th in the world in the percentage of young people between the ages of 24 and 35 with a 4-year college degree. And there is one reason and one reason only: We tripled the cost of getting that degree while incomes remained flat. And it has been going on for 30 years now. The delivery system is fundamentally flawed . . . This is a prescription for our economic downfall." Something's got to give.

Where else does the expense side of our personal budget get out of control?

Dev lost his Visa card when it fell out of his pocket during a run one day. After calling to get a new card, he had to actually look at all the things that were being automatically deducted each month: Highrise, Vimeo, Dropbox, Skype, Netflix, Base-camp, YouSendIt, Mad Mimi, Shopify, and HootSuite, most of which he never used. It was amounting to over $150 a month. It was a wake-up call that lots of us need, unthinkingly hemorrhaging money on nights out, impulse purchases, late fees, ATM fees, cab fare when we could walk, the list goes on and on. Each dent in your bank account may seem insignificant, but these little frivolities add up. Identifying those vacuums is the first step toward regaining control of our finances.

When he was a child, Dev's parents bought a coffee table book called *Material World: A Global Family Portrait*, in which the photographer, Peter Menzel, traveled to 30 countries to take a picture of one statistically average family with all of their possessions. What people lived with was poignant in its range— the Natamo family in Mali with their mortar and pestle, the Ukita family in Japan with their television, toys, and treasured jewelry. Each family had full lives, and seeing the material things that sustained all they did made the point that it was possible to live with less. A lot less.

Dave Bruno attempted to do this in North America. He started a mini-movement when he decided to cut his possessions down to 100 things, which he tracked online and in a book with a challenge to others to do the same and discover the simplicity, joyfulness, and thoughtfulness that resulted. What would you lay out in front of your home today if you had to live with just 100 things? What would be the first 100 things to go? Maybe today is the day to start simplifying.

Simplifying can be an empowering act. Simplification can also come from knowledge about where our money actually goes.

Tracking our finances and actually knowing where we are spending money can be a daunting prospect, but if you really want to begin managing your finances better, figuring out what it costs you to live each month is a great start. Services such as Mint.com have good online software that can help, but you can also just create a spreadsheet to track your expenses.

Try this: For 1 week, write down every single item that you bought. Carry a notebook around to record cash expenditures. Then reflect: What was a requirement for life? What could I happily have done without? What does that say about my relationship to money?

This is hard to do. It's usually not just laziness that prevents us from actually doing this; it's because confronting the truth and the great unknown of our expenses makes us anxious. We're afraid of what we'll discover. Just knowing can begin the act of regaining control and revisiting our relationship with money.

We can start to identify ways to reorganize some of the major expenses in our life. Sixty percent of people's incomes is spent in just four areas: housing, transportation, utilities, and healthcare. Are there changes in these big areas that could be a game changer for your budget? The growing sharing economy—which includes car sharing, co-working spaces, couch surfing, children's toys, and clothes swaps—gives us good options for cost saving, and some have the added benefit of helping you meet other like-minded people.

Reconsidering how we structure our relationship to consumption is precluded by a healthy, conscious relationship with money. The rules we learn about money have been largely passed on to us by our parents or early childhood experiences. Exploring what these are for you is important. Ask yourself: What are your beliefs about how money should and can be made? How should it be spent or given away? And where did these beliefs come from? These questions and the subsequent personal exploration will lay the foundation for a stable and healthy relationship that will provide you with the freedom to do more—to invest in your friend's start-up, take a career risk, travel, or do whatever else you'd like.

WHAT DOES DOING GOOD MEAN TO YOU?

Billy
The early days of my environmentalism were hard on the people around me. A recent convert to vegetarianism, I turned evangelical, pressing friends and family to defend the ethics of the hamburger they were about to bite into.

Worse, at least as far as my friends recall, was my attitude toward shampoo and deodorant. My arguments rested as much on an embrace of my natural odors as they did on the (scant) environmental benefits of not using the products. Others did not embrace my odors. My freshman-year roommates, Yoon from South Korea, Yaw from Ghana, and Omar from Lebanon, all impeccably hygienic and scented young men, just didn't understand. What ultimately broke the boycott was a bad scalp itch that found me at a dermatologist, who told me that my scalp looked like those on the homeless men he treated. He prescribed a medicated shampoo, and sent me on my way with a friendly but stern, "Wash your hair, son."

Over the years, as I found more effective ways to make change on these issues that I cared about, I downplayed the "lifestyle environmentalism" critiques. I became focused on the political and structural barriers to solving the climate crisis, and I started washing my hair. I saw that we needed to build a movement that was positive, aspirational about the future, not one that made people feel bad about themselves.

I also began to recognize a division in the broader environmental movement that mirrored my own. Alex Steffen, founder of the Web site WorldChanging.com, has popularized a framework for the way the two major camps in the environmental movement, bright greens and dark greens, view the future. His definitions are worth quoting:

> "Bright-green environmentalism is a belief that sustainable innovation is the best path to lasting prosperity, and that any vision of sustainability which does not offer prosperity and well-being will not succeed. For the future to be green, it must also be bright. Bright green environmentalism is a call to use innovation, design, urban revitalization, and entrepreneurial zeal to transform the systems that support our lives . . .
>
> Dark greens, in contrast, tend to emphasize the need to pull back from consumerism (sometimes even from industrialization itself) and emphasize local solutions, short supply chains and direct connection to the land. In its best incarnations, dark green thinking offers a lot of insight about bioregionalism, reinhabitation, and taking direct control over one's life and surroundings. In a less useful

way, dark greens can tend to be doomers, warning of (sometimes even seeming to advocate) impending collapse."

Of course, many of us have elements of both the bright and
dark green worldviews and have struggled with doubts about
one path or the other. Skeptics of the bright green path hear
"sustainable innovation" and think "capitalism and technology," and wonder how the forces that got us into this mess are
going to get us out of it. And skeptics of the dark green path
point to the facts of human nature, our habituation to certain
creature comforts and massively growing population and consumption, and see a futile behavioral challenge.

To be sure, the bright greens bring a lot to this party. Who
wouldn't be excited about putting supercheap, nontoxic, thin-
film solar technology on the roof and getting paid for the electricity that it produces? Don't most of us want to hang onto our
cars and MacBooks, but just wish they were designed to be sustainable? After all, there's no reason they can't be. At the same
time, there's no question that we, too, need to change and evolve,
to "be the change we want to see in the world." Most of the dark
green changes we should be making—eating less meat, biking
and walking more, or bringing our own mug, for example—
would not only reduce our footprint, but also make us healthier
and happier. Fortunately, there's a campfire somewhere between
the two sides that is attracting an increasing number of people
who believe we can and must embrace both. Van Jones has given
us a unifying rallying cry: Green Jobs. What's so powerful about
the idea of Green Jobs is that it addresses our fundamental need
for work and income, while it also contributes to solving the big

environmental challenges we face. By definition, a Green Job both makes money and does good.

In asking "How do we do good?" each of us needs to develop a theory that can evolve with the work we do. How do you think your career and actions will impact the world around you? What result will your actions have? What unintended consequences? No theory of change is perfect or the only way forward, but taking a hard look at what you care about and how you can do something about it will help you know your role.

So many of us complain about our jobs and never ask ourselves "What do we really care about?" That disconnect between the work we do and where our hearts are makes it hard to find reasons to show up every day. Work as a data analyst has little to do with the time spent with loved ones. In fact, our work is often the very thing that prevents us from having that time from which meaning is derived.

It wasn't always this way. Before the Industrial Revolution, humans spent a good portion of their time on activities directly related to survival—to the food that we gathered from the land or the clothes that we made to keep warm. Once we began to civilize, our work was predetermined by our gender, our class, our race, and our place of birth. We did what our parents did, whether we liked it or not, and we kept the same job for the duration of our lives. Most people didn't sell their time; they sold and traded what they produced—be it food from the family of a farmer or shoes from the family of the cobbler.

The Industrial Revolution changed everything. People began to sell their time for money, which enabled them to buy other things, creating a wedge between what we need to live and where our time and work go. This gap makes it harder to make the connection between the work we do and the reason we do it. It makes it hard to see the direct connection between our work and its effect on our health and environment.

Today that gap is so huge that people can defend and justify the work they do as a data analyst at a large oil company, while also worrying about their own child's asthma. Our personal lives and our work are often at cross-purposes, and the actual impact of our work is often so remote that it is natural not to take responsibility or feel conflicted. Instead, we just complain.

What we may be truly complaining about is the gap between the random, meaningless work so many of us do from 9 to 5 and the ideals that we hold dear. Today there is a shift occurring; an increasing number of us want work that actually provides more than just money. Work should make visible the connection of the hours at our job to our health, our lifestyle, and to the things that we want for our family and ourselves. This type of work doesn't make us feel like complaining and/or feeling desperate for some way to escape for the weekend, but affirms us and motivates us by the very nature of how synchronous it is with what we care about.

Are you doing good in your work right now? Doing good is about living with compassion, principle, and awareness to the positive impact you can have on the world. For years, Billy kept above his desk a small clipping from the *New York Times* about Arthur Winston, a Los Angeles bus maintenance worker who had retired on his 100th birthday after three-quarters of a century working for public transit agencies. He never called in sick, was always on time, and missed only 1 day in his whole career, back in

1988 when his wife of 65 years passed on. He could have retired in his early seventies but kept working to help family members who were struggling financially or pursuing college degrees. He planned to keep busy by doing charity work and taking advantage of his free bus pass to explore the city. "I'll be on the move," he said. "I'm not going to sit and mope in the house."

Each of us has to define what a meaningful life means—it's always going to be different, depending on our unique combination of interests, skills, experiences, and worldview. Growing up outside Los Angeles in the 1920s, Arthur Winston found a sweet spot with the Los Angeles transit agency that allowed him to help provide affordable transportation for millions of people and support his family. You will surely have your sweet spot to find, but you'll also need to be prepared for the sweet spot to change, as the world changes and as you change.

Doing good doesn't have to be about working for a nonprofit, it doesn't have to be about feeding hungry people in the Third World—it can be about finding purpose in helping people each day live their life better. Everyone has to make a unique contribution, a passion that fits with the life you want, the family and friends you have, and the world that you want to create. It also doesn't usually mean you need to start up your own thing. We need Rebuilders in every level of the transformation of our society.

At the same time, we also have to recognize the little and big ways in our own lives that we continue to be a part of the big problems the world faces. Our world is organized to make the cheapest and most convenient methods to eat, buy things, and power our lives unhealthy for us and unsustainable for the planet. Every time we leave the water running, leave the lights on, or simply travel from one place to the next, we make an impact. Our actions, when taken collectively across billions of people, have enormous implications.

Given the enormous challenges facing the world, many of us will need to step it up, to be leaders, and to help remake the world. Our collective future rests on this, particularly in the rebuilding of the enormous sectors that sustainably meet our most basic needs for food, energy, mobility, shelter, education, connection, and more. As Bill Drayton, the founder of Ashoka, says, "Our job is not to give people fish, it's not to teach them how to fish, it's to build new and better fishing industries."

HOW DO YOU WANT TO SPEND YOUR TIME?

Recently Dev saw a tableau in the men's room that seemed to capture our twisted relationship to technology and time. At the urinal was a businessman texting avidly, both hands on his BlackBerry. As Dev walked out, he wondered if we really have become so busy that we can't spend a few minutes in the washroom without having to fire off a quick e-mail.

Our time is being nibbled away on a thousand fronts, all under the guise of making us more effective, more organized, and more connected. Whether it's a quick status update on Facebook, the slide down a chain of related YouTube videos, or compulsively checking our inbox, our ability to manage time has vanished, leaving us floundering for control.

As we zip through our lives balancing several tasks on the head of every moment, we often get 15 things done without any progress on the one thing we actually need to do. We're always working, always plugged in, but rarely do we feel productive.

Consider the squirrel. Squirrels only ever find and eat

30 percent of the nuts that they hide. They spend almost all of their time running around, gathering and hiding nuts so that they can be sure they'll have a nut on hand when they need it. In a lot of ways, technology has many of us acting like squirrels, running around, busy all the time working on stuff we hardly ever use. What would happen if we slowed down and really optimized the time we spend working so that it yields nuts we end up eating?

The demands of our schedules have many of us booked solid. Often this lack of free time stops us from trying something different, taking a creative risk, or experimenting with a more efficient workflow. Knowing that you may not have the flexibility to rethink your whole schedule, let's start with a small change in rhythm we call Permission Time.

Scheduling Permission Time is a beginning practice that can reclaim moments from the smear of the day, an hour today or an afternoon tomorrow. It should be scheduled with the same importance and intention as a meeting with one's boss—not to be missed, not to be moved.

Start by giving yourself an hour. For that hour, you have permission to forget all of the things you have to do, everything that is weighing on you and, most important, everything you are supposed to do. In this hour, you have permission to do exactly what you want. It may involve writing a note to a friend, going for coffee, drawing in the sketchbook many of us keep and neglect. It is your hour, and you have permission, control, and agency over what happens.

Schedule as frequently as needed. The effect should be grounding and rejuvenating. At first, you may find yourself taking Permission Time to grab a coffee, take a nap, or zone out, but what will happen if you continue the practice is you will start to look forward to that hour in your afternoon for a more focused reason. That hour will help you generate more ideas for what you love to do, get more creative work done, and propel yourself into the rest of your day reengaged and reinvigorated.

Does the idea of committing to an hour away from your schedule make you nervous? Why are we afraid of unplugging, of what it would mean to take an hour and do whatever we like? Perhaps it's because we're worried that if we step away, we'll miss something crucial, that we'll fall behind past the point of being able to catch up.

How would you feel if someone offered you 5 days by yourself on a small island off the coast of British Columbia in the middle of a busy time of year? Eager to get away? Nervous at what you'd miss while you were gone? Dev was both when he was dropped off by motorboat, given a kayak, a tent, and enough food and water for 5 days. He spent his days thinking, drawing diagrams, and trying to catch fish out of the kayak—there wasn't much else to do. His context, a literal island, gave him permission to completely turn off for a few days, and when he came back, he felt a new energy and insight at work.

Can you let yourself just be there in the moment, waiting for the restroom, folding laundry, making a sandwich, or do you feel like you need to have your e-mail window open and the phone on speaker? What are you afraid is going to happen if you take 10 minutes away? Answering these questions and looking at your relationship to downtime will create more breathing room in your suffocated calendar, enabling you to make better use of your working hours.

There's scientific proof that mental rest from our work and gadgets, an introspective state neuroscientists term "default mode network," is important for brain function and for a developed sense of self. Think of the difference between ruminating on your day, letting memories and associations ebb in and out, noticing the way things look and move around you, versus constantly receiving little snippets of information and never having time to assimilate it. We need time to think away from the glow of our screens.

Even more than simply being present, find space in your life for some kind of mindfulness practice. Mindfulness can take lots of different forms, from a physical practice like tai chi or yoga, to guided imagery meditation, to simply experiencing the sensation of your breath coming in and out of your body, noticing your thoughts but letting them pass without judgment. Research shows that some types of meditation actually change the structure of our brains, producing long-term cognitive benefits that impact stress levels, your memory, your imagination, your attention span, your ability to empathize, and your overall happiness.

There are also some technological tools that help us "get away" just for a little while. Internet-disabling programs like Mac Freedom recreate the feeling of an island by shutting off your online connection for a period of time that you determine. It gives us just a breath of space to do our work in, enforced protection from the appeal of the Web. Another approach is to simply limit yourself to two dips into the e-mail inbox per day. Try it for just a week; if you check your e-mail for two 1-hour sessions each day, you're more effective at actually replying to e-mail, rather than watching it pile up.

At the 2011 Women of the World conference, Arianna Huffington told a packed auditorium how much she valued and respected her sleep and how ridiculous it was that men bragged about how little sleep they got. The night before, a dinner companion had bragged about only getting 4 hours of sleep each night because of how busy he had been. "You know what I wanted to say to him?" Arianna asked us in her thick Greek accent. "I wanted to say, *If you slept for another few hours, this conversation would be much more interesting.*"

The dinner companion in Arianna's story is a product of this story of ego we have built that sleeping less is a good thing. Many of us buy into this cultural myth that taking downtime means being lazy or indulgent, that you build a strong career on the broad back of a 100-hour workweek. But, in fact, downtime is one of the most creative and generative parts of our day. Doing less will enable us to do more.

There isn't a set prescription for the amount of downtime we all need every week or what you need to do to get it. In fact, your needs and abilities will probably change and evolve with your own schedule and stress level, but one thing all of us can work on is the quality of our time.

We all have that friend who is there in the room with you but whose mind is distracted, somewhere else, not present. Often *we* are this person; even when we're alone, our mind is racing through work or weighing our stresses. This is why quality downtime has two factors that are in your control: presence and permission.

Permission time, idle time, *it's all well and good*, you might say, *for a person who has nothing better to do*. But you have hours, undiscovered hours, and we're going to help you find and reclaim them by showing you how to say no and regain a reverence for your time. We can wrestle back control of our time and consciously spend it on the things that nourish us, the things that support the way we want to live, and that help us build our careers that both make money and change the world.

Time is a unique resource in that it is both abundant and nonrenewable. When we use a unit of time, we have not reduced the amount of time available. When we use a minute or hour or day, it does not change the fact that there will be another minute or hour or day immediately after. If we were to be killed in an instant, the next second will arrive nonetheless. Even our reckless consumption of natural resources and pollution of the environment will not allow us to consume time. In this sense, time is abundant.

Yet time is also nonrenewable. Once we use a minute, we can never use that minute again. It is gone forever. Time is the most valuable thing we have, so how we choose to spend it matters a lot. How people spend their time varies enormously from country to country. Over 16 million times a day somebody in Japan sings into a karaoke microphone. Millions of low-income women around the world spend 20 hours a week just collecting water from distant rivers or wells. Americans spend 34 hours a week, equivalent to a second full-time job, watching television.[1]

The average father spends twice as much time in a car as he does with his kids,[2] but if you polled most fathers, none of them would say they care twice as much about their '06 Hyundai Accent as they do about the warm-blooded kids waiting for

[1] Nielsen. *State of the Media Report*. Rep. no. Q3 2011. Nielsen Media, 2011.

[2] Robbins, John. *The New Good Life: Living Better than Ever in an Age of Less.* New York: Ballantine, 2010.

them at home. But remember what Adrienne Maree Brown says: "Actions express priorities." We've gotten ourselves into structures and routines that devalue our values—they simply aren't a factor in how we book our time.

Ask yourself: *"How closely does how I actually spend my time fit to how I'd like to spend it?"*

The first step to answering that question is understanding where your time currently goes. It takes some bravery to inspect yourself this way, to really answer for yourself what proportion of your waking hours goes to things that ultimately aren't that important to you. But to do that, you first also need to dig into the second step, which is understanding what's actually important to you.

Often our ability to assign urgency to something is flawed, and we feel we must do something because we'll feel guilty if we don't, or because we want someone to like us, or because it seems like an impressive thing to do, or because everyone else is doing it, or just because we sort of feel like it. An amazing transformation can take place when you begin tracking where your time goes—we can move from scattering our energies without any design at all to life where we are only spending time on the things that make us feel guilty if we don't do them. How? It happens when we learn the one time trick and efficiency hack that will never underdeliver and will always free up enough time for you to focus on things that are important to you—*saying no.*

So simple, yet as we all know, sometimes it's the hardest thing to do.

LEARNING TO SAY NO

1. Understand the ask. Understand what you are saying no to and what you are saying yes to. Often we don't take the time to clarify exactly what we are signing up for. Do this first. Make sure it is clearly communicated exactly what you are signing up for, and you may even realize you can say yes to something that you initially didn't want to do.

2. Ground yourself in yes. By knowing what your priorities are, by differentiating between things that feel urgent and important and things that actually are, we can find the power to say no. In moments where you have to decide, your declaration of what you are saying yes to—what you want in your life—will give you the confidence to say no.

3. Don't make excuses. It can be so easy to make up an excuse, to create an on-the-spot alibi, or to simply say yes without the intention of following through, letting your future self deal with the consequences. Don't do it. Stick to what you know, what you have already said yes to.

DAILY PRACTICE #4: INNER KNOWING

In what ways are we imprinted with understanding from life events? From the time we almost crashed when first learning to drive, to a moment we were moved by an incredible gesture of kindness, to the first time we discovered someone had lied to us, the experiences of our lives are etched into our brains. Sometimes these gut reactions are good and worth trusting.

But sometimes, depending on our experiences, they can also lead us to unhappy results.

Inner knowing is about a smaller, more quiet voice than just your initial gut reactions. Often, we bury our true understanding in rationalizations, secondary points of view, the pros and cons, and overanalysis. We actually know the answers to the questions we struggle with. All too often, we either fail to consult our inner understanding or we disregard it because we feel like we don't have a choice.

This discipline will help you understand and decode this quiet inner voice and give you access to the wisdom you already have. It will help you make better decisions. This practice will help you to create more results, with less energy and less thought, and will subsequently help you feel less stressed out about those never-ending serious questions that demand answers.

The practice starts with a question you want to ask yourself. Big decisions like:

* What do I need regarding my health issue?

* What's the right strategy for _____?

* What do I need to do about my problem with _____?

* Do I take this career opportunity?

Practice with the many little decisions. As we learn to trust ourselves on the small decisions that we make each day, big decisions will come more easily. Small decisions like:

* How can I make this telephone call most successful?

* What food would best serve me at this meal?

* What should I do with this unexpected 15 minutes of open time?

* What do I need right now?

To begin understanding the shorthand of your inner voice, it helps to follow four steps:

STEP 1: CENTERING

Our minds are always racing through thoughts and ideas, obscuring our ability to hear the inner voice. The unquiet mind makes ripples on the surface of the pool . . . the image is distorted. Sit still, take a bath, meditate, and center yourself. Quiet your mind to bring your deeper knowing into focus.

Do not proceed to step 2 until you are relatively centered.

STEP 2: ASKING

Direct attention inward, into the place where your experience is centered. Eyes may be closed if this helps you focus. Ask a simple, direct question. Choose your questions with care. Be precise about what you want to know. You will find an answer for exactly what you ask for.

STEP 3: RECEIVING

Remain open and nonevaluative. Responses may come in many forms: words, images, a felt sense of knowing. Pay particular attention to what you receive immediately after asking. The first information or response is usually the clearest. There will usually be a wave of clear information. Notice when this is over, and you begin to think, analyze, or evaluate what you first heard. Stop the process as soon as this shift occurs. Record what you received accurately. Take care not to add, omit, or interpret what you "hear" at this point in the process.

STEP 4: APPLYING

Do you understand what you received in response to the question? What else do you need to know? Formulate your next question with as much care. If needed, recenter yourself.

Repeat steps 1 to 4 as needed, until you feel resolved in your answer. For more complex decisions, consciously walk through each of the steps. For smaller decisions, simply ask inside, using these guidelines to separate inner knowing from mind chatter.

The key to evaluating the reliability of the information you receive is to focus on the feeling you get when receiving it. Don't get lost in the voices of your internal critic. All your moods, passing notions, and subpersonalities have read the same books you have. With time and practice, you come to recognize your own inner knowing—it's like learning to recognize the voice of a new friend over the telephone. A few tips in sorting out who's who:

1. Be wary of anyone in there trying to sell you anything. The inner salesman is almost always a scam artist. Inner knowing has a "just so" quality to it. No hype.

2. Self-important, inflated voices are not inner knowing. They are the result of pride.

3. Self-judging, self-critical, or harsh voices are not inner knowing. They are the result of insecurity.

Remember, you get what you need to know, not what you want to hear. We are often seeking a kind of control that is not real. Inner knowing invites us to just listen, in an act of radical trust. For example, we often want to know about the future out of anxiety—not because there's anything we actually need to do right now. The practice of inner knowing most often lets us know what we need to know right now.

Often when you don't get an answer, it's because the way you have asked the question may not be answerable or you may be resistant to hearing the truth. Our answers may come as visual images or in the way our body physically reacts. And sometimes, answers may come later from outside ourselves—from other people or events, from "coincidences," signs, or from nature, which, often in spite of ourselves, we take as evidence of a truth. You will come to know, love, and trust the voice of your inner knowing. It speaks with the energy and qualities you would like to have more of in your life: clarity, compassion, and authenticity.

Like all of the disciplines, inner knowing is strengthened by repetition. If you start using it regularly, even many times a day, as the word "practice" suggests, it becomes habitual. You will begin to understand the shorthand of all your learned experience, and your wisdom will be more and more available, increasingly without even asking.

So remember: Consult and listen to your inner knowing before making each and every decision, large and small.

RESOURCES

* Resource Generation is an organization based in New York that helps young people with privilege leverage their resources for social change. The book Classified (by Karen Pittelman & Resource Generation) is a great primer that helps anyone ask the basic questions about where our ideas about money come from and what they mean.

* The Virtues Projects based in Canada provides workshops and a series of books that help explore the role of virtue in our daily lives. The book The Family Virtues Guide (by Linda Kavelin Popov with Dan Popov, PhD, and John Kavelin) provides a path and structure to talk about and cultivating virtues within a family context.

* Hollyhock Institute is a progressive retreat center based in British Columbia that offers a series of retreats and programs that range from sessions with Robert Gass to sessions on modern dance, all grounded in an understanding of self and sustainability.

* Books we love:

    * *Ishmael* by Daniel Quinn

    * *The Portable Coach* by Thomas J. Leonard with Byron Laursen

    * *Deep Economy* by Bill McKibben

    * *The Great Turning* by David C. Korten

    * *The Green Collar Economy* by Van Jones

    * *Siddhartha* by Hermann Hesse

CHAPTER 5

ADAPT

"The only constant is change."

—Octavia Butler

Lynn Hinkle had worked 30 years on the rivet line at the Ford Ranger plant in St. Paul, Minnesota, when rumors began to circulate in 2004 that the plant was closing down. More than 2,000 workers were slated for layoffs—Lynn included. Many at the plant had spent the better part of their careers on those 350 acres spread along the banks of the Mississippi, and now they were being forced to imagine moving on. A union task force formed, and Lynn jumped at the opportunity to mobilize his fellow workers.

Lynn and the rest of the task force tried to convince Ford to consider restructuring manufacturing and keeping the plant open, but the conversation went nowhere. The international union supported the effort but didn't engage. Ford slowly started laying people off. As his co-workers began to lose their jobs, they came to Lynn's office and shared their despair about life after the shutdown. He began to hear day after day about his co-workers' lack of opportunities for any other work and their fears that everything they had learned and accomplished would be irrelevant.

Lynn had heard about green energy technologies—solar, electric cars, and wind turbines—so he went to the community to learn more. He began reaching out to student groups and to community organizers. Together with people he met doing his research, he began to put together a plan for a mixed-use redevelopment of the property, for the conversion of the plant into one that produced electric vehicles.

In the middle of a meeting in which Lynn was presenting his plan to Ford and members of the community, a man stood up at the back of the room and challenged him. "Who are you to be telling us that we need to transform this plant?" the man asked.

"Let me tell you," Lynn replied. "Let me tell you about the hours I spent standing on a shift with my ears bleeding because of the rivet gun, let me tell you about the workers who came into my office afraid of what else they'd lose when they lost their jobs. And let me tell you how I have searched and I have simply found no other place that can provide these jobs we need other than the emerging green economy."

Lynn's experience, insight, and flexibility had given him strength and pragmatism that revealed his opponent's position as a knee-jerk backlash to change. He had seen the inevitability of change and had taken action to reinvent himself to meet it. He let go of the constrictions of habit, opened his mind, and, leveraging the foundation of his experience on the rivet line, educated himself to make himself an essential player in a world prioritizing sustainability.

In 2010, as Lynn stepped into a completely new role as

policy director for the Minnesota Solar Energy Association, Ford proposed repurposing the factory to produce its first battery-powered vehicles. When his way of life was headed for the wall, Lynn created new work for himself by adapting and helping Ford understand that its future depended on adaptation too.

We need to adapt. The reality is that the days of full-time, long-term, office-bound employment for many of us are probably numbered. Independent workers already make up 30 percent of the nation's workforce.[1] This sector includes freelancers, consultants, independent contractors, temps, part-timers, contingent employees, and the self-employed. The biggest opportunities to make money and change the world will come with unusual job titles and hours. Many of the best jobs 10 years from now probably don't even exist today.

Human labor is being replaced by technology so fast that workers can't keep up. Whole cities across the United States have been hollowed out by the loss of manufacturing jobs that began with the pursuit of a financial- and information-based economy in the early 1980s. Outsourcing jobs overseas has spurred growth and employment in China and India and many other countries, helping to bring tens of millions out of poverty. And yet, the world faces the highest level of recorded unemployment in history, with no end in sight. We're making babies faster than we're making jobs.

Digital technologies are fundamentally shifting the employment picture across virtually every sector. Look at retail: With

[1] *Freelancers Union.* www.freelancersunion.org.

the rise of online shopping and self-checkout counters, 1 in 10 Americans employed in the retail sector are facing a bleak future. Skill sets required for many careers are in transition too. Nurses and doctors are just beginning a massive digitization of their work, which brings incredible gains for accurate diagnosis and good cures, but also an evolving set of Web-enabled tools that health practitioners will have to learn to use.

We have a lot of work to do. The imperatives of the real world are pushing us to open ourselves up to change, to be flexible enough to get the knowledge we need to thrive. Labor markets are shifting, and we see the battle between people struggling to hold onto old careers and those trying to embrace new ones playing itself out across the entire economic spectrum.

Adapting is hard. We have a deep desire to stay comfortably where we are, without risking the turbulence of the unknown. We mainly perceive change from the perspective of hindsight, and when we consider the sweep of its timeline and the very gradual manifestation of its results, making an immediate step toward initiating change can seem too small a gesture, almost futile.

The comforts of familiarity aren't always the best indication of whether we are doing the right thing. Often, they prevent us from opening up to good change. The comfort we find in familiarity can make it difficult to make space in our routines, to take that leap into a new career or a trip abroad. The familiarity of a steady paycheck can make it difficult to take the risk necessary to start a new venture.

But what are we giving up when we prioritize comfort in our decision making? Baby Boomers have given us thousands of examples of what happens when we settle for the safety of stasis rather than risking change. In fact, most of us probably don't have to look farther than our homes or schools to find stories from parents or mentors who have hit a crisis point where they wish they'd chosen a path that inspired them from the beginning.

In fact, as the children of the Baby Boomers launch into careers, many of us are also seeing our parents start new businesses, learn new trades, and get involved in local organizations. A research report released by Civic Ventures identified that half of all adults ages 50 to 70 say they are interested in taking jobs now or in the future to help improve the quality of life in their communities. Some still need to earn income, some want to stay connected to the people in their community, but above all, they want to maintain or find a sense of purpose in their lives.

Our ability to adapt at the same pace as the world will enable us to identify society's problems and needs, build our own corporate ladders, while still providing the security we all fundamentally need.

During his first year at college, Dev was skateboarding down a concrete path on a steep hill, coming back from a late-night math class. Averaging a pretty high rate of injury on skateboards, he wasn't altogether surprised when he wiped out. But he was surprised to hear what the doctor treating his dislocated shoulder later told him: If only Dev had been drunk, he wouldn't have gotten hurt. It was all that tension colliding with the concrete that dislocated his shoulder. If he'd been more relaxed, loose, and flexible, he might have rolled with the fall and emerged unscathed.

When we resist change, we become anxious, we tense up. Sometimes we can live our whole lives in this state, holding fast to our known skills, our known network, our known job. But what happens when our industry shifts and we're downsized?

Or something causes us to suddenly look around and realize we can't stand what we do for a living anymore? If we're inflexible and resist change, chances are high we will hit that proverbial wall and dislocate something. And as Dev can attest, that's a painful experience.

Being flexible, adaptable, and open to change is a core tool for survival in today's fast-changing world, where the professional skills needed 10 years ago aren't what's needed today.

There are many personal reasons we resist the idea of adaptation. Maybe we've tried new things and they never seem to work out. We may have tried to apply to grad school, but we didn't get in. We may have retooled our resumes and tried for a new kind of job, but it didn't work out. We tried once, and when things didn't work out, we gave up.

Our expectation for instant results is a type of impatience that affects our willingness to try something different. We cultivate that impatience in part from success stories made famous on the Internet, on TV, and on the cover of magazines. These are the stories of the one person in a million getting discovered on YouTube and finding worldwide fame or a tech entrepreneur starting his company on a whim and selling it after 6 months for $100 million. The easy glamour of these stories makes us feel that if it doesn't happen in 6 months, we are doing it wrong, and it's not going to happen for us at all.

Dev uses a simple idea to fight the impatience he sometimes feels when he inevitably runs across a 1-minute success story in the media. Gary Player, the famous golfer who dominated the game in the '60s and '70s, made a seemingly endless number of lucky shots. He explained his style this way: "The harder you work, the luckier you get."

But it is easy to ignore that simple idea, and every day you can find examples of people copying the wrong things. They buy expensive golf clubs and forget the practice, hoping that luck and instant results actually exist.

Undesirable situations become comfortable over time. We have choice: Adapt and seek comfort in the familiar and undesirable, or we can push ourselves into new territory, adapting as we go.

Traditionally we've relied on education to arm us with the training we need to become versatile, adaptable candidates, but in reality, formal education can instill in us a kind of passivity—we answer only the questions given to us, feel good only if we get a good grade, and wait for someone to tell us what to think about.

In the stories of the Rebuilders we interviewed for this book, we found that successful adaptation in the real world hinges on two principles: open-mindedness and learning mastery. Open-mindedness is a deeper attitude than willingness to try exotic foods; it means truly releasing aspects of your identity that no longer serve you, approaching significant life events with a cool-headed appetite for growth, spending time alone at the right moments to sift truth out of the static of experience. It helps you adapt by prioritizing the truth and possibility in new information over the safe, narrow comforts of what you already know.

Mastery requires self-knowledge and patience, both hard to come by in our instant age. But putting in the work of building and mastering skills makes us resilient candidates for jobs in a time when the skill sets needed across a variety of fields are constantly evolving.

OPEN-MINDEDNESS

If you want to be open to adapting, you can't presume to have all the answers. As soon as you presume to know something, you stop listening to learn and start listening to prove yourself right. The truth is always repositioning itself no matter how "right" we are at any given point; a million metrics are shifting, changing the picture.

Many people experience being truly open-minded for the first time while traveling. By stripping away the familiarity of our routine and our home, we begin to look at seemingly every-day things with a curious eye. We ask questions that we would never ask about our own cities and entertain thoughts that alter our direction. We are inquisitive, sometimes even happy, to get lost, come into new ideas often, and eventually settle into a sense of calm as we navigate our changing environments. Trav-eling inspires the kind of spontaneity and heightened aware-ness that we need to replicate in our careers.

We can also begin to gain a sense of openness by refresh-ing our orientation toward our routines. Haruki Murakami, in *What I Talk About When I Talk About Running*, writes about the rolling procession of thoughts and mental blankness that can arise in a repetitive act like running—he calls it "acquiring the void." He quotes novelist W. Somerset Maugham, who wrote, "In every shave there is a philosophy." No matter how banal the routine, there is an opportunity to be astonished, find insight, discover new questions, and learn something new, one we often don't find the presence to claim.

Being open to new ideas can also come from the practice of allowing yourself an unexpected yes. Instead of sitting at home, go out. Instead of going to the restaurant you always go to, try going to a lecture that interests you. Search for a fresh perspective, a new set of eyes. Uncover the layers of your routines, remember why they became habits in the first place. It won't always be a light bulb moment and, in fact, you may find that you rediscover why you have your habits. Start by simply looking and noticing, and feel the shift in your reaction.

There was a three-word message inscribed on a yellow promotional pencil Dev picked up at a conference: *It is possible.* What a simple concept. Dev took a few pencils and kept them on his desk to produce the same effect as the experience of letting an unexpected yes slip into his daily routine—it reminded him not to shut down ideas that seemed silly or weird or out of sync with his patterns. It is possible that I will actually enjoy hanging out with a new group of people, or that I can learn how to build a Web site using PHP, or that I will actually be able to survive a game of pick-up soccer without embarrassing myself. It is possible.

The key to finding that openness to possibility is cultivating an awareness in three critical scenarios: when we feel ourselves clinging to something mainly because we're accustomed to it; when an experience jars us with its poignancy or its challenges; and when we're all alone, confronting the truth of our lives. In each of these scenarios, there are opportunities to choose an openness that trains us in the art of adapting.

LETTING GO OF OUR NOTIONS OF SELF

We can easily find ourselves in prisons that we have constructed for ourselves, fixed identities that limit the scope of our activities.

What do you define yourself by? Have you always been the person that gets good grades or the person who does the research in a group project? Have you always been the leader in the group or someone who waits for others to organize?

Letting go of something you define yourself by can open your eyes to all kinds of new opportunities. When we cling to our set notions of what we're good at, we run the risk of becoming afflicted with tunnel vision when it comes to opportunity. We opt out before giving ourselves the chance to compete. The nonprofit careerist sees only the opportunities for programs and foundation grants, and the industrial designer thinks exclusively of the product that can be created. Clinging to a limited definition of who we are as workers narrows our possibilities.

If we are able to actually let go of that single, defining label—banker, organizer, painter, whatever it is—and wake up the next day realizing that life goes on, that you still have the power of your experience, knowledge, relationships, and personality, failure can provide a deep sense of confidence.

The Rhodes Trust offers one of the most prestigious scholarships in the world, where each year, a select group of leaders receives a full scholarship to Oxford University and a lifelong network of previous recipients, some of whom are Nobel laureates and presidents of countries. The Rhodes Trust practices this idea, encouraging scholars to grow by shedding their old identities.

Near the first week of the scholarship, all of the scholars are pulled into a room and given the following commands. You've all gotten here because you have been focused on sports, your academics, or your leadership—and because of that, you may not have had a chance to do other things. Be social, explore a different area of study, travel. This is your chance. Explore without the fear of failing.

It's rare that we're presented with such an invitation. To fail, to try out completely new things and shed, even for a short period of time, the things that have come to define us. Our prisons can be wonderfully comfortable, but there is another place for us to go. We have to leave behind the security of who we have become and set off to become the person we have the power to be. We don't need to wait for anyone to give us that permission. We can make the choice ourselves.

Ask yourself: *"What identities and labels do I cling to? What would happen the day after I left them behind?"*

TEACHABLE MOMENTS

John Francis was 25 and working as a volunteer firefighter in Marin County when he heard on the news that two oil tankers had collided on a foggy night in the San Francisco Bay. He drove down to the bay with his girlfriend to witness the 840,000 gallons of oil that had spilled into the waters. "I couldn't get away from it," he says. "You could close your eyes, you could turn around, but you just couldn't get away from the impact of it. The smell was overpowering." The spill killed 10,000 birds, whose bodies were littered across oil-coated beaches. It took 5 years for the tidal life to once again find an equilibrium in the area.

A year later, he lost a close friend, and overcome by the fragility of life, he decided to act on an idea that he had originally joked of when he witnessed the spill. He stopped using motor vehicles. No planes, cars, buses, trains. Just his two feet. The act was in part based on the hope that others would do the same, but instead, he found himself in relentless argument and debate with those around him. So 1 year after committing to only using his feet, John decided to not speak, to not defend himself anymore, and to just listen for a single day. And then another, and another.

For 17 years, he communicated only through improvised sign language, notes, and a banjo. Without speaking, John completed three college degrees and a PhD in land management at the University of Wisconsin at Madison. By the time of the Exxon *Valdez* disaster in Alaska, John had become one of the nation's leading experts on oil spill cleanup. He was recruited by the US Coast Guard to write oil spill regulations and by the United Nations Environment Program to serve as a goodwill ambassador. John wrote later in his book *Planet Walker*, "I had no idea that I was going to become a UN ambassador, I had no idea that I would have a PhD, and I realized I had a responsibility to more than just me and I was going to have to change."

John's path was determined by choices he made in response to powerful experiences. But we all have experiences, large and small, that simply pass us by with no lasting impact. Dev's parents raised him using a concept they called *Teachable Moments*. The idea was simple: Wait until a life experience presents an opportunity to learn, and then try to extrapolate a broader meaning from the event. Discuss with friends and family and reinforce the lesson.

Searching for the lesson to take from one of these moments can sometimes seem like an artificial search for a silver lining: *What should I learn from this massive failure?* That question is usually the last thing you want to hear when something bad happens. But teachable moments don't always arise from massive failures. In fact, the best ones often arise from small everyday events—decisions you feel a twinge of anxiety about or an off-handed comment that makes you reflect on the truth of who you are.

The concept of teachable moments isn't just a parenting tool for 5-year-olds, but also a useful way to shake off the paralyzing feeling of being overwhelmed by all we don't know. We don't need to know everything before we begin. Teachable moments require you to go beyond asking, *What should I learn?* They require you to also ask, *What should I do next?* Direct. Action-oriented. Your answer will not only give you the next step you need, but it will be grounded natur ally upon the right lesson arising from that moment. John didn't know where that first decision to stop using motorized vehicles would take him, but he had the courage to take the first step down the road that led to powerful professional experiences.

SOLOING

Billy

To date, about a half dozen times in my life, I've done something that strikes many people as odd or scary or insanity-inducing: I've gone off to be completely alone in a forest for days at a time. This practice began with an opportunity that came up during a high school semester at the Mountain School in Vermont to spend 3 days and nights camping alone. The kids on the trip each had their own gorgeous spot of woods at the headwaters of Reel Brook in the Kinsman Range. We were given a big orange whistle to blow if we ran into trouble. Every morning, we'd go down to the stream and raise a little green flag, which a teacher would later come around to check and lower. Save for the flag, we were all alone to be wild and weird, to run and shout, get naked, build a sleeping fort, and watch the animals or bugs or the flowing brook.

Being 17 and truly alone with myself for the first time in my life was a self-discovery like no other. The high-stakes feeling of being a teenager made the epiphanies hitting me feel pretty epic, and you can see from my journals that I was chiseling out some bold new opinions in my time alone:

Morning of Day 2: "Joyce Carol Oates' tirade 'Against Nature' is worthless. I can't imagine a person who wouldn't be moved by time alone in the woods. There is a reason why Thoreau spent time at Walden Pond, why Chris McCandless went to Alaska, why the United States preserves national forests, why [The Mountain School] sends its students into the wild. There is an ancient bond between humans and nature, where the meaning comes from is immaterial: it is there; it has always been there."

Afternoon of Day 3: "For the first time in my life I feel like a man. Going on this solo, taking charge of every aspect of my life and doing okay was the missing rite of passage toward manhood. I feel entirely prepared to take responsibility for myself; I feel prepared, upon hearing a whistle blow, to run as fast as possible to that person to lend a hand. I am entirely independent and I feel this freedom in every action . . . I expect that I will use the strength, confidence, and independence gained on this solo to be more self-reliant."

I had lived, played, and gone to school almost entirely within a square mile of the Upper West Side of Manhattan. I had doting parents who proofread my papers for school, cooked my meals, and otherwise took care of all my material needs. More than my high school graduation, more than my confirmation at church, those 3 days were a coming of age.

Many of the students at the Mountain School were from cities, and the idea of 3 days alone in the woods was alarming for some. We had read a little of Thoreau's *Walden* and also *Into the Wild*, the true story of Chris McCandless, not much older than us, adventuring on his own into Alaska by himself and never making it out. But we all made it out, and we saw each other and ourselves with new eyes. There were some things we shared passionately, and others kept private, unexplainable still. The solo meant different things for everyone in the class, but everyone seemed to emerge more confident, purposeful, mature, even wise.

The summer before my freshman year in college, racked with anxiety about the impending separation from my then-girlfriend, I secluded myself in my grandfather's Pennsylvania cabin to track deer, read Marquez and Eco, and think about who I was and where I was headed.

After a solo during Thanksgiving break in my sophomore year of college, I brought a new energy to my activism that got almost half the Yale campus to sign the "Eco-Pledge," saying they wouldn't buy products from, work for, or invest in 10 big companies (Pepsi, Staples, CitiBank, etc.) until they took specific steps to reduce their environmental footprint. We started crashing their recruiting sessions, raising the stupid, bad things they were doing, and turning away potential Yale grads from jobs with their companies. Quickly the message filtered up, the companies freaked out, and many of them did exactly as our campaign demanded.

The summer in India, feeling alone and struggling with the poverty and environmental degradation I saw there, I found solace and direction on a few long, mountain hikes. I came back from India burning to make change.

Solitude is a lot like sleep—it's a quiet period when our mind regenerates. If sleep is when we physically rest, recover, and grow, moments of solitude are when we mentally recover. In solitude, the pressures we all face from modern life are walled out, and we are left to reflect on our experiences and make sense of our ideas, learn about ourselves, and grow from our conclusions.

A good solo is actually not very hard to pull off. You don't need a parents' second home or money to travel to a far-off locale. Even just a full day and an open mind to really consider and explore what's going on with you at the moment can change your life.

Fully disconnect. No Internet, no phone, no quick status updates telling people "It's *so* amazing to be alone!" The setting matters some too, so take a little time if you can to ask around. My best solos have involved a lot of time outside and in nature, but you should have good equipment and may need to ask a friend to check on you if you're gone more than a couple days. Set aside as much time as you will need, but recognize it will likely take a day or two for the effects to begin to set in.

The personal discovery and growth you can achieve on a solo can give you that flexible edge you need to shift, adapt, and be open to changing direction. Often, we don't know what's wrong in our lives until we're completely alone, without a schedule or outside voices, without spikes of competition or envy—simply unspooling thoughts, reflecting, really probing ourselves for hypocrisy, dissatisfaction, longings, and disappointments. In those discoveries, there's an opportunity to right our path.

LEARNING MASTERY

After graduating from the University of California, Santa Cruz, Arthur Coulston got a job at the local bookstore and volunteered with the newly formed California Student Sustainability Coalition (CSSC). When the need arose for a Web site, Arthur stepped up. He didn't actually know how to create one, but echoes of his father telling him he could do anything he wanted to prodded him along.

He asked the tech guy at the bookstore to give him a little primer, and the first thing he learned was how to find the markup of a Web site, the underlying code of how the site was designed and built. If you can see it, Arthur knew, you can learn it. Weeks later, he had designed a basic Web site for the CSSC, and by the time he was done, he'd learned so much that he started another one from scratch. And then another, and another. Still superbasic stuff, but enough for a statewide student network with a couple hundred members.

So when Billy first met him at the founding meeting of the Energy Action Coalition in the summer of 2004, Arthur still wasn't exactly a pro. Arthur signed up to be on the Web site committee, and, again, just kind of got to work. Using his natural design inclination and a lot of learning by doing, he started piecing together a Web site for the Energy Action Coalition. He got good at finding answers on Google for the best way to do whatever we needed—it was all out there to be found, usually within 5 minutes.

By the time the coalition had money to hire for the position, he was the clear choice. He was already doing the thing we needed someone to do. And several years after he stopped working for the coalition, when Dan Rosen and Billy were looking for a co-founder for Solar Mosaic who actually had some tech skills—not another generalist entrepreneur who can plan, pitch, fundraise, and partner—they turned to Arthur. And again, Arthur delivered—this time, creating a beautiful online marketplace for solar energy.

That willingness to commit to giving it a go not only makes people like Arthur adaptable job candidates, it also gives them practice in the art of trial and error, a key aspect of adaptation. Mastering a skill takes both discernment and patience. We have to start with truly knowing what it is that we want to learn, and we have to be prepared to put in the time. The following tips are designed to help answer the two questions that inevitably came up for the Rebuilders we talked to: What should I learn? And how should I learn it?

WHAT DO YOU ALREADY BRING TO THE TABLE?

We read a lot of "how to find a job" books while writing this book, but our favorite was the 100-page, no-nonsense *The Job-Hunter's Survival Guide* by Richard N. Bolles, author of probably the most famous career guidebook of all time, *What Color Is Your*

Parachute? Bolles breaks down the relative effectiveness of different job-hunting techniques, pointing out that mailing out resumes, answering ads in newspapers, or searching online job boards are all only effective for 10 percent of people who use those methods.

Bolles lays out the single most effective technique this way: "Do homework on yourself, taking inventory in detail of all you have to offer and what you are looking for." Simple advice, but something we actually rarely make time for. Here are three sets of questions to sit with, to reflect on, and to launch you into the process of discovering the skills and traits that you might not have realized you already have:

1. What are some of the things you're good at and love doing? These can be specific (writing grant applications) or general (math).

2. What were your biggest challenges or major life milestones in the past 5 years? What character traits did you employ during these important moments? What were you able to learn from them?

3. What environments bring out your best self? Do you prefer doing office work, being outside, or working from home? Do you prefer working by yourself or in groups? Do you want to be working in the place you're living now, or are you feeling drawn to another location?

Before focusing on what new skills you want to master, it's important to get a good sense of both the foundation of skills and traits you already have as well as the kind of job or work environment you can be happy applying yourself to.

EXERCISE: BUILDING YOUR COURSE PACK

Dev

When I was in my first year at university, I began to rip out arti-cles that I found interesting. I ended up picking up profiles of people—ranging from a short interview with a graphic designer I respected to a list of 25 people I dreamed of emulating one day. I would rip them out and throw them in the bottom drawer of my desk, unconsciously and without an agenda.

Eventually when I moved out of residence and came across the stack of clippings, they reminded me of the multisource course packs I spent so much time with in college. In the inter-est of getting organized for the move, I took all the clippings to the copy center on campus, photocopied everything, had it bound with a plastic sheet on the front and cardboard on the back, and threw out my originals.

The course pack sat on my desk, and as I flipped through it semiregularly over the next few years, it became an invaluable resource. It was both a source of inspiration and a do-it-yourself instruction manual for the things that interested me most. It was filled with interviews with people I looked up to and those short how-to articles that you normally read, find interesting, and forget when you need them most. Over the years, the guides I've made have been a vital reference, always at easy reach to scan and send an article to a friend, and as I look back now, many of the people I had put in the course packs have become close colleagues and friends.

STEP 1: GET A BOX

It can be a plastic bin, a cardboard box, or a large drawer, but whatever it is, keep it close to your desk.

STEP 2: CUT OUT

Cut out any articles you find that are interesting and relevant to your passions and throw them into your box. Watch the pile grow. Create a folder in your browser bookmarks specifically for this purpose as well, saving the URLs of the articles that you love. "Cutting out" can happen both on and offline.

STEP 3: COPY SHOP IT

After 6 months or so, take the box to a copy shop and photocopy each article, note, or picture so that you have a stack of 8½ by 11 paper that can easily be bound and read. For the online articles do the same—print them out and take them with you. Sort the articles however you like and ask the copy shop to bind the packet with a hard cover on the front and back.

STEP 4: READ IT

When you're bored or looking for inspiration, flip through your course pack and make notes in it. Leave it on your bookshelf. Memorize the people, reread your favorite articles when you need a little inspiration, find the patterns, and follow up on leads that you find hidden in the articles. Rinse and repeat—I now have 10 of these booklets on my shelf that I still read through regularly and refer to often.

The Four Paths to Mastery

Arthur geeked out on the powerful tools that enabled him to build an online platform that empowered a youth movement to work together, to share, to really see each other on an ongoing basis. It started with a pet project he'd work on nights and weekends, and that set of Web site design skills became the source of his livelihood *and his passion* for a decade, at least so far.

We have both gotten a lot of mileage out of this basic approach—picking up skills like facilitation, grant-writing, training, public speaking, media engagement, coalition-building, and graphic design because they were essential for the organizations and companies we've helped lead. But we're also grateful there are people, like Joel Rogers, who have deeply studied the problems we face and have generated the research, knowledge, and ideas that can contribute to scalable solutions.

Joel is a professor of law, political science, public affairs, and sociology at the University of Wisconsin at Madison. In addition to 10 books, Joel has written nearly 200 reports and articles (almost all available online), and he has helped start dozens of influential sustainable economic development collaborations over the years. He's also a MacArthur genius and has been identified by *Newsweek* as one of the 100 living Americans most likely to shape US politics and culture in the 21st century. These accomplishments, and this impact, would have been impossible without the training he received in college, law school, master's and PhD degrees, and decades of academic research.

If the academic path to mastery isn't for you, it can be extremely beneficial to have mentors or colleagues who have this depth of mastery over your field of interest. When Billy was working out the original idea for the Clean Energy Corps program to put people to work retrofitting and installing solar on buildings across the United States, he went to Joel for help.

Joel wrote the original white paper and provided much of the intellectual rigor the proposal needed to get the endorsement of over 100 major national organizations as well as the presidential campaigns of Hillary Clinton and John Edwards.

So now, consider this question: *What is the one thing that I need to learn right now?*

To truly master a skill, we need to be more than just good at something—we have to be actually excited by it so that we make enough time actually doing it. Mastery is, to a large extent, about the time you dedicate, so a good way to discover what you want to become masterful at is asking yourself: *"What really interests me? What would I never get sick of?"*

If you haven't yet, take a minute to name something you'd like to learn.

Where do we go from there? How do you go about mastering it? After an initial self-discovery of purpose, almost all of the people we talked to followed one of a small number of paths to mastery:

* Worked for a company or organization

* Apprenticed for someone they admired

* Researched, learned, and taught themselves

* Went to school to get some specific training and an essential credential

It's up to us to pick which path we use to instruct ourselves.

It can be hard to get motivated when we weigh all of the factors implied by learning something new—career relevance, free time, or potential for greater money. Maybe our decision can feel like a reaction to outside circumstances, the easy decision to seek safe harbor in school while you figure things out. Sometimes these feelings are justified and even necessary, so which method do you need to use to learn right now?

DAILY PRACTICE #5: DEEP LISTENING

"We have two ears and one mouth so that we can listen twice as much as we speak."

—Epictetus

Real listening is rare. Just trying it for a few days can transform your experience in the world. To adapt, we need to be aware, and we need to listen in order to remain open-minded, find those teachable moments, and develop the mastery we need to become employable. The discipline for this chapter, Deep Listening, will help you cultivate that awareness, and you will find as you begin the practice that it is as much about listening to others as it is about listening to yourself.

If we don't listen, how can we communicate, build relationships, or learn? It's amazing just how often we don't listen to the people around us, whether they are close friends or someone we are meeting only casually. We get the gist, or we let our minds wander, or we plan what we're going to say in response. This discipline gives you the chance to experience what it's like to actually listen—how different the world seems and what you can learn when you pay close attention.

Deep listening costs you nothing, but can dramatically change the way you lead, change your friendships, and change your intimate relationships. When people don't listen, fissures of mistrust develop in our organizations, our communities, and our relationships. Our ability to solve, to create, and to move past the challenges of our times requires that we learn to listen to each other. Try it for just 1 day, and you will see why.

STEP 1: BEGIN LISTENING

Starting today, with each and every person with whom you speak, bring the deepest and most respectful quality of listening. Hafez, a 14th-century Persian poet, explained the idea beautifully: *Listen to each and every person's words as if they were the cherished last words of your most revered teacher.*

Take notice of your own thoughts as you begin to listen. When you feel them drifting off, let them go and bring your complete attention back to the person in front of you. Whether you are talking to the person at the grocery checkout aisle or to a friend you haven't seen in a long time, challenge yourself to be truly present and listen to everything that is said.

STEP 2: SHARPEN YOUR PRACTICE

Deep listening demands us to be present. To really listen, as you may have already experienced, it's as if you are zooming in your attention on the speaker, rendering the rest of the world a blur. Notice how listening is much more than just hearing. A study at UCLA found that up to 93 percent of communication comes from nonverbal cues. So "listen" to the body language, the visual context, the facial expression.

LISTENING HABITS

LESS-SKILLED LISTENERS	SKILLED LISTENERS
Immediately evaluate what is being said	Suspend judgment and listen
Spend time rehearsing what they will say next	Focus on what the other is saying
Try to steer the conversation	Let the other person direct the conversation
Hear everything through their own frame of reference	Try to enter the other's frame of reference
Ask questions to satisfy their own curiosity or interests	Only ask questions when the other seems to need help
Disagree with other's point of view	Seek to understand other's perspective
Try to take in and respond to everything	Sort for main ideas
Allow their mind to wander to other things	Keep focused on the other and the other's words
Parrot back exactly what they heard	Reflect back the essence/feeling of what was said
Give little verbal and nonverbal responses	Actively encourage speaker through verbal and nonverbal cues

STEP 3: MAKE IT PART OF YOUR ROUTINE

Commit for 1 week to following through on this practice, listening deeply to all the people in your life. Change the notification when you turn your cell phone on to "Listen!" Write it on your hand, on your computer, next to each appointment in your agenda—wherever you know you'll look before you talk to people.

No matter how many times you have done this practice, you will find there is always a way to access a deeper level of listening, a new set of knowledge, and a new outlook on once-familiar relationships. The more you practice, though, the more habitual this kind of listening becomes, and the deeper relationships you'll be able to build.

RESOURCES

* Learning from each other, as we once did, is catching on again but this time it's online. There are a number of sites and resources that are leading the way, including: Skillshare, Udemy, Academic Earth, and Instructables. They are all great platforms that help you learn and teach anyone from anywhere.

* There are a number of companies that provide opportunities to go abroad, volunteer, and make a difference. One of our personal favorites is run by friends and is called Operation Groundswell. They are nonprofit, committed to learning from the places they travel, explore environmental sustainability, and only work on community requested projects. Check them out at Operationgroundswell.com.

* The Massachusetts Institute of Technology (MIT) is at the leading edge of the movement to provide university level education for free with their OpenCourseWare. They provide lectures, notes, and video tutorials from their undergraduate and graduate curriculum free of charge to all online. The Open University, based in the UK, has a similar mission and is also worth looking into. Private companies like AutoDesk are also providing free sustainability training at sites like sustainabilityworkshop autodesk.com.

* The most famous and well-curated "big idea" Web site is TED.com but there are also others such as The Big Think or RSA Animate that are worth checking out for inspiration, ideas, or to learn something new.

* Books we love:
    * *The Art of Thinking* by Ernest Dimnet
    * *Astonish Yourself: 101 Experiments in the Philosophy of Everyday Living* by Roger-Pol Droit
    * *Encore* by Marc Freedman
    * *The Teenage Liberation Handbook* by Grace Llewellyn
    * *Dumbing Us Down: The Hidden Curriculum of Compulsory Schooling* by John Taylor Gatto

CHAPTER 6

CONNECT

What you know means nothing—it's who you know that counts. You have to grow your web of connections. Plan maps of the six degrees separating you from everyone you admire. You need to collect more business cards and go for more lunches. It's all about "golden rolodexes" and networking events, loose connections and high connections, warm contacts and cold contacts. Tweet constantly. Friend everyone in sight. You need to be a maven, a connector, a network hub. Get an extra smartphone to keep track of all your connections.

This is the absurd way we have come to envision what it takes to build a network. The whole production has become so stressful and soulless it makes many of us want to take to the woods.

Whether we learned these lessons from a success coach or simply gathered them by osmosis, the advice around building professional networks and connections leaves most of us feeling overwhelmed, uncomfortable, and a little like that wheeler-dealer we probably don't want to be. We can feel anxious and pressured just going on Facebook, where we involuntarily compare ourselves to people with more "friends" than us. But is it productive to have a gigantic network of people you have no bond with, people you know only because they're "useful"? And isn't seeking people out in this strategic way an affront to our natural impulse to connect genuinely with people we like and care about?

When we think of the conventional notion of networking, it can feel like a self-serving activity stripped of conscience and conscientiousness, a kind of ugly, raw ambition. Networking is so misunderstood, so overly strategized that the whole prospect of meeting people outside of your group of friends can feel like a big turnoff. What am I even going to ask people? What do I have to offer? I don't have anything to promote, so what's the point of meeting anyone? What am I supposed to say—can I have your card? It's usually after that awkward excuse to end a conversation that most of us decide to just stay by the bar and hang out with the few people we already know.

Dev

In the summer of 2010, I began working with the Pepsi Refresh Project, which used a democratic online process to give out millions of dollars to anybody with a specific idea to do good. The competition was open to people in America and Canada, and the marketing tagline was "Refresh Everything." The program itself was created in partnership with GOOD/Corps, an LA-based consultancy that I worked for, and had the effect of positioning Pepsi at the cutting edge of companies that were transforming their marketing budgets toward philanthropic ends. Pepsi was seeing both the financial and social benefits sync, and it was exciting to be a part of it.

The projects and ideas covered a range of issues, and there were thousands of entries each month. You not only had to enter at the exact right moment, but you had to be pretty strategic about building a campaign and mobilizing voters in order to win the money. Competition was fierce, yet somehow one small town of 15,000 in upper New York state had won multiple grants totaling more than $350,000 for a handful of local organizations.

It was because of this that I ended up in Cohoes, New York, in October of 2010. Cohoes used to be a bustling industrial town, powered by the Mohawk River and the Cohoes Falls. It used to be known as "Spindle City" for its large textile mills. It was booming in the 1800s. Then industry moved on, and as people moved with it to urban centers across North America, the town became largely abandoned. Large buildings lay vacant, Main Street was filled with facades that held the outward appeal of their early 19th-century roots but were empty inside. The county music hall, the bank, the post office, the police station, the church, the school, and Main Street itself were at some point deserted, a familiar story for hundreds of towns across North America. The pieces were there, but they needed rebuilding.

Almost 100 years later, Cohoes is getting its second chance, and I saw it firsthand. The theater was unboarded and taken over by ex-Broadwayers Tony and Jim. They leased the theater for a dollar a year from the city, mobilized the community, and started to win grants and bring in money. They held professional stage productions, bringing in actors from Broadway, while providing programs for local youth. The former Cohoes Bank was bought by a young couple, Alana and Jesse, and was being rebuilt as an arts space called the Foundry for Art, Design + Culture, their expenses partly covered by big parties they threw when they first moved in. There are plans for empty parking lots to be turned into urban farms, and a new generation is moving back just as local residents are stepping up.

The mayor, whose family has run the town pharmacy for decades, was at the bar the first evening I spent there, and over a pumpkin ale, he shared the potential, the ideas, and the way the community was enabling the rebuilding to happen. A 5,000-square-foot building on Main Street can be bought for $80,000, and that gets people talking. As we walked down from the theater, Jesse, the now-owner of the old town bank building, pointed at buildings and vacant lots. "We want to turn that into an urban farm," he said. "The owner of this building gave us the keys so we can use it when we hold large arts events. We want this to once again be a hotel. We figure it's possible to buy it, and Tony and Jim from the Music Hall will be able to support it just through the actors who are coming through town already."

They banded together as a community to support each other in the process of rebuilding everything. Jesse and Alana applied for the Pepsi Refresh Project and began rallying the community for votes. They won, and it opened up the idea to others in the community to apply. They cobbled together a network founded on real relationships—the result is allowing them to rebuild an entire community and feel good about each other too.

Our culture celebrates the myth of the individual achiever—in sports, business, politics, culture, and even movements—we tell stories of heroes who accomplish incredible feats on their own. But we know this isn't how things work. Michael Jordan won his six NBA championships with the help of about a dozen other players, from all-stars like Scottie Pippen to clutch "sixth man" players like Toni Kukoc. Aung San Suu Kyi, the Nobel Peace

Prize–winning leader of the democratic opposition movement in Burma, derives her power for change from the countless individual acts of bravery from the millions who work for freedom.

This isn't to take away from the powerful courage, creativity, and leadership these individuals have demonstrated. In fact, these leaders, like any good leader, would be the first to admit that their accomplishments were only possible with a whole lot of support, from parents to coaches to friends and colleagues.

Billy and Dev's work, similarly, has been a result of collaborations and support from hundreds of people of the Energy Action Coalition. Virtually all of the 20 people at the founding meeting played a critical role in bringing it to life. When Billy needed to move on, Jessy Tolkan and Kassie Rohrbach were there to take the coalition to new heights. For Dev, it would have been impossible to launch and build the technology that drove DreamNow's business if it wasn't for his friend Edward Keeble. If there were an acknowledgments list for our careers, it would fill pages and pages.

The point here is simple: We're stronger together. Relationships are the foundation of solid careers and powerful movements. But what kinds of relationships? And how has technology altered the way these relationships come together?

The way we understand networks has dramatically shifted, as previously invisible relationships have not only become visible, but transparent. Our network of connections has become part of our daily parlance. These networks are not only creating new ways to start and keep contact with people, they also seem to be promoting a culture of reciprocity, generosity, courtesy, and mutual support. We follow each other, "like" each other's updates, and note each other's inspirations.

That culture makes us inclined toward service and helping, not because we expect something in return, but because the positive climate of our community makes us want to cheer people on. Sure, the Internet is rich with negativity, with haters who anonymously troll around and want to see everything fall to ruin, but much of what happens online shows that we're inclined toward goodness, toward building a reputation that makes people want to keep us in their lives and in their network.

The challenges we face today are so huge and complex that we actually need to work together. We need to take our newfound network visibility, our desire to genuinely connect with others, and combine them with the lessons that have always worked in order to build new networks on strong foundations.

This chapter is about these types of relationships. It's about building a powerful support network through authentic connection driven by our genuine desire to collaborate, to care, and to help those around us. This network will very likely be your greatest asset on the Rebuilder's path—helping you identify opportunities for work, raise money, build a customer base, and providing coaching and emotional support when you most need it.

We'll explore different strategies you can use to build that natural network, using methods you probably already employ in your healthiest, closest relationships—focused attention, a desire to see other people succeed, and reciprocal support. We'll also look at how to avoid negative influence within our networks and how to really light up the switchboard when we need our connections to get behind us. In today's changing landscape, it's more important than ever to create a network that feels less like work and more like home.

THE INTENTION IS THE MESSAGE

In his 1964 book, *Understanding Media: The Extensions of Man*, Marshall McLuhan explained the idea that we should be focusing study on the medium itself. For the past 50 years, this notion has governed much of how we understand communication. If we look through this lens today, we can see that we are living in a new world, inundated daily with voices streaming in from different mediums—text messages, Facebook walls, e-mail, Listservs, video chats, and the occasional ringing phone. Each of these gets used for personal messages, group messages, and spammers alike, which has devalued the effectiveness of many of our mediums to actually connect.

Media static has caused a lot of confusion about the best way to get a message out. Should I buy a banner ad or e-mail my alumni list? Should I post a Facebook status or a YouTube video? Should I host an event or Chatroulette my message onto the HP monitors of unsuspecting strangers? In spite of our confusion about the best medium for messaging, today the energy and sincerity of a message is exponentially more important than its medium. The genuine energy in a message's design will help it connect with an audience, making the type of platform you use to launch much less important.

We have collectively developed the ability to sense authenticity in just a few characters. Though how to know when someone is being authentic or self-promoting is not part of our formal education, we know right away. Our whole set of life experiences has accrued to teach us to quickly calculate the sum of the energy, the expression, the tone, the gestures, and the words themselves and to judge whether or not someone is being genuine with us. You know the difference between someone

honest, smart, and on their game who actually cares and someone who is "networking."

So how do you ensure you are communicating the right
intention? First, you actually have to care about what you're
communicating. There's no way to fake that. When you reach
out to people in your support network, you have to be doing it
for a reason that you feel good about.

Beyond that: Imagine each letter, Facebook message, note,
or text you send not delivering the words themselves, but rather
delivering the feeling and intention behind the message with
100 percent accuracy. Imagine you are following up with a business leader you met at a conference but with the sole intention
of asking for money. You send a simple e-mail along the lines of
"It was a pleasure to meet you, let's stay in touch. I would love to
get together." Now imagine that the words actually communicate your intention: to get money from the company. How
would your communication change? Would you write at all?

Dev did an experiment that ended up showing him the
importance of authenticity in communication. He decided that
he would send 50 postcards to Facebook friends he felt discon-
nected from as a way to reconnect and deepen the relationship.
As he began to write, the messages were filled with the intention of surprising his friends, of making them laugh, or telling
them that he cared about them, but as he started to burn out on
the project, he reached a point where he found himself just fir-
ing off quick, low-energy notes. He kept track of which ones
he'd written when he had started to feel like he was writing on
autopilot. He sent them all out at the same time.

A few weeks later, he began to hear back from some
people—a quick message of thanks, a couple pieces of mail,

a mix CD, and what ended up being a recommendation for a contract. The vast majority of these replies came from the individuals that he had written to at the outset of the project, when his mind and heart were present for the production of each individual piece. People sense genuineness, and they respond to it.

Try this to immediately feel the difference intention makes in communication: Read the phrase "How are you?" as if you were in the following situations:

As if you were reconnecting with an elementary school best friend—"How are you?"

As if you were a police officer checking in on a wayward civilian—"How are you?"

As if you were a businessperson trying to sell another product—"How are you?"

The differences in tone and warmth here show the difference between sending a quick note without thinking about why you're doing it and imbuing a note with the intention that you want to communicate. You will write differently, and the recipient will perceive that difference.

In short, communicating with intention means communicating with caring, which translates into a deep consideration for the person receiving your message.

THE MAGIC QUESTION

The secret to really having an impact in your world and building a network that will support you lies in a single question. It's a question you don't even have to ask aloud; rather, you simply have to act upon it: *How can I help?*

Helping doesn't necessarily mean what you think it does. It doesn't have to take a huge amount of time, and it's not about giving your services away for free or doing something you don't want to do so that you can ask for a favor in return. No one ever built a real friendship just by sending a person birthday e-cards. True help builds an ebb and flow of reciprocity, without self-serving expectation. It's actually a whole lot more natural.

Think about how it feels when someone encourages you, shows you an opportunity you may otherwise not have seen, or simply keeps you top of mind when meeting interesting new people. If you want to build a network that actually supports you, you need to build a network of friends not connections. A network that you care about who they are, not just who they know.

Billy

My sister and I were driving out of Zion National Park after finishing a beautiful hike up Angel's Landing when an unexpected message popped up in my voicemail from a guy I'd grown up with, but who'd never really been a close friend. Ben Bronfman had gone to Emerson College after high school but, like me, had left before finishing. His dad was a top music executive, and Ben had a ska-punk band called the Exit that had a growing following. His message was refreshingly direct.

"What's up, Billy. It's Ben. We haven't talked in a while, but I've just been thinking a lot about global warming, and it's freaking me out. I know you've been doing something with the Energy Action Coalition, and I want to help."

A few weeks later, we got together for a walk around the

reservoir in Central Park, and I told Ben about how the coalition had just launched the Campus Climate Challenge, and more campuses were signing up every day to run the campaign. We had a big budget and were growing fast, but we had been having a hard time piercing the pop culture and mainstream media bubbles. We started brainstorming ideas and how we could work together—how Ben might bring some of the relationships and experience he had from the music industry to match the distribution network we had built with the Energy Action Coalition to reach our generation.

About a year and many conversations later, we had formed Green Owl Records together with a producer and sound engineer named Stephen Glicken and set as our first project a compilation CD with all proceeds going to benefit the coalition. The Green Owl Comp had Feist, Muse, Bloc Party, and a bunch of other popular bands, and we were able to sell 20,000 copies online and at the checkout counters at every Whole Foods in the country.

In the end, the Comp didn't make much money for the coalition (overhead costs needed to be paid back), but it did accomplish something even greater; it got us a ton of press, helped us grow the profile of the coalition, and gave us the cool factor we needed to land a big partnership with MTV a year later for a new campaign called "Break the Addiction."

Since the day of that phone call, Ben and I have become great friends and worked on a number of other projects together. From a simple offer to help, relationships can grow with the power to transform careers and the world at large.

There are four components to the kind of help that builds a friendship network rather than a rolodex:

*   Find the right person at the right time.

You can't plan in advance how to help people effectively. Real help comes from providing the right thing at the right time to the right person. We do this naturally as long as we listen and seek to really understand each person that we spend time with. The better you understand, listen, and grasp what they are dealing with, the easier it will be to trust ourselves to filter all that information and provide help when needed.

*   Be an opportunity scout.

At some point, you may meet someone who seems to be doing something very similar to what a friend is doing, or you may run across a book that speaks to exactly what they are dealing with. Think of yourself as a scout for your friends, out there in the world helping to look for answers to their questions.

In the same way that you make notes for yourself when you stumble upon a good idea, when you find a piece of advice or even a simple idea that you think would actually be relevant to your friends' needs, send it off to them. You can write a two-line text or even a quick e-mail, but the most important thing is that you pass on the contact, idea, or compliment when it comes to you. The actions don't have to be major, or even incredibly regular, just relevant and useful.

*   Follow through.

Nothing is more frustrating than when someone says he'll do something for you and doesn't. Even if it's something small like a link you said you would send, each time you fail to make good on your promise, it degrades the belief people have in your ability to follow through, and it slowly fractures the relationship.

*   Create your own culture.

Building a network is a culture-building activity. Workplaces have cultures, nations have cultures, and our networks take on a culture. Your actions can precipitate a feeling of either reciprocity or selfishness, and it is up to you to decide whether you want to foster a spirit of collaboration and emphasis on real bonds, honest relationships, and trust or whether you want your relationship to be about numbers and business cards. The culture you create will be what you live with, what sustains you, and what enables you to unlock the resources you need to build your career. You decide what kind of culture you want to create.

PEER COACHING

Billy

For someone like me who sometimes vexingly answers questions with questions, never allowing the focus to linger too long on my own problems, the peer coaching I participated in at the Rockwood yearlong training was a revelation. For a couple months at a time, we were paired with a peer, and we scheduled calls every 2 or 3 weeks to talk through what we were dealing with at work and in our personal lives. This model gave me permission to share my needs freely, to feel heard and cared for, to be supported and challenged to look at things from a different perspective, and to dig deeper and try to really understand the roots of my troubles.

Finding the right person (or people) to be a peer coach is the first, and often the hardest, step. It can be anyone you trust and have an affinity for, and it doesn't have to be someone who knows everything about your industry. The industry-experienced type of coaches are useful as they can save you years of trial and error and enhance your effectiveness by sharing the history in the field—but they aren't always necessary.

But today, when we are in the process of rebuilding everything, when we are living in a constantly shifting job environment and building careers in industries that didn't exist 10 years ago, a good coach could just as easily be someone that's a really good listener, who supports you 100 percent, but whose insight into your field may come from an outsider's point of view.

If you can, try to cultivate multiple coaching relationships. Chances are you need support in many different areas of your life—everything from your career to your spiritual path—and most of us won't find that support in a single human being. Another benefit of having a team of coaches is that it gives you the freedom to construct your own path while still getting the wisdom of multiple perspectives. When there is only one person you are checking in with, you may start trying to emulate that person too much, and you can be distracted or misled from your own unique path. Having a balanced team of friends that you can check in with will help you find the support and insight you need to keep on building, growing, and creating.

We all have some of these kinds of relationships already—with family, friends, teachers, or co-workers—but it can make an enormous difference in the quality of the support you get (and can offer in return) when you formalize the relationship and bring some basic structure to the coaching sessions.

Although friends may be doing some of the same things for us, without formalizing the relationship, you don't have the permission to share all of your problems in a one-sided way. As friends, we tend to jump in to conversations sometimes more focused on how what our friend is saying enlightens something about our own experience, instead of spending the time holding up the mirror for your friend, asking the right questions, and helping them gain clarity.

Once you have identified the people you really want as peer coaches, here are a few key tips to get the most out of those relationships.

1. MAKE THE ASK

Start with a friend or colleague, someone you have chemistry with and have known for a while. Tell them about what it means to be a peer coach, how the benefits are mutual, and how it can be an on-off thing or, if it works, a more extended commitment. Treat it as an experiment—a chance to gain some understanding and share some of the challenges you are wrestling with right now. It works two ways—so you both get a chance to share. Propose some clear expectations for the relationship, and since you want to be able to really open up, an agreement to respect privacy and confidentiality is a must.

2. LEARN TO LISTEN AND ASK POWERFUL QUESTIONS

We all know the difference between good and bad listeners. Bad listeners these days often come in the form of the at-the-table BlackBerry addict, but classically they're the ones interrupting you, constantly turning the conversation back to themselves, or glancing over your shoulder. While we all get annoyed with bad listeners, many of us were never actually taught how to be good listeners ourselves. As it turns out, there's a true art and science to good listening. Revisit Daily Practice #5: Deep Listening (page 159), and here are a few additional tips specific to peer coaching:

* It is your responsibility as the one listening to ask the right questions. Before you give your own opinions, you want to invite the person you are speaking with to explore for himself the problems and solutions to what he's struggling with. *How* and *What* questions often invite creativity and new possibilities. *Why* questions can be the most powerful but can also put the speaker on the defensive and, if asked unskillfully, may take a coaching session off track. Consider the following coaching questions:

  • What do you think that was about for you?
  • How did you do that?
  • Why do you think it turned out that way?

* You may not always get to be in person, but the nonverbal cues can make a big difference. If you aren't in person, try video chatting—seeing the person can really help communicate that you are paying attention, that you care, that you are present, and that you are fully listening.

3. SHARE THE RESULTS

You don't need to take all the advice from all coaches, but it is important to tell them if you did use their advice and if it worked out. Following up with results is a wonderful thing for coaches to hear, and it's the ultimate in acknowledgment for a voluntary act. It also helps you show them that you are not only listening, but that you are committed to integrating what they share with you into your own life. It also helps both partners become better coaches, improving the probable effectiveness of future sessions. Talk about what worked best in the coaching session, what you're going to take away and act on. Let them know if there are things you'd like to try next time or if there were suggestions that didn't work.

SET POINT

The concept of Dunbar's Number, which we began to discuss in Chapter 2, arose from a study based on primate groupings, which predicted that humans could only maintain stable social relationships with an average of 150 people. After the dawn of the Facebook era, Robin Dunbar went back to the drawing board, analyzed new research culled from social networks, and came to essentially the same conclusion. Despite the fact that people may keep thousands of online "friends," the average number of people they regularly communicate with is still around 150.

So how important is the makeup of our 150? Miguel de Cervantes said, "Tell me the company you keep, and I'll tell you what you are." The people who fill our lives determine a great deal about our identities and the design of our existence—what we think is normal, good, worthwhile, and doable. We call that foundational community your Set Point. Think of it as your resting heart rate, the pulse that exists to support you with minimal effort. It is our default setting.

If most of your Set Point is resigned to working at unsatisfying jobs, you might subconsciously learn that all that exists in the world is work that leaves you unfulfilled. If your Set Point sees the world as full of opportunities, resources, and money, you will subconsciously learn that the world yields to support worthy projects.

Your Set Point accrues over time: a few from school, others at work, some at parties, each a layer added to the bedrock of friends and family who seem to have always been there. It can feel like we don't have a lot of control over the people who make up our Set Point, but, in fact, we do make choices about who we invite into our network and who we spend time with. In many ways, these choices flow from other choices we make about our work, education, our love life, and our spiritual paths.

For both of us, it's not just Rebuilders who dominate our network. Of course, we've both found a beautiful community in this work and built many close relationships with fellow Rebuilders, but there are also those who come from a different perspective and contribute to the mix of ideas that push and challenge us. What's important is that your network supports you and stretches what you believe is possible just by the way they live.

Your Set Point can be shaped and transformed by seeking out and joining communities that already exist. If you want to be surrounded by green builders, start with research. Look up the local chapter of the Green Building Council, learn the specialized language and terms the builders use, and find out who their leading thinkers are and where they speak and convene. Half of joining a community and transforming your Set Point is just showing up to the right place.

One hundred fifty is a satisfyingly large number, but the

number of people in our daily mix is often a lot smaller. These are the people who know us best, who are intimately engaged with our ongoing goals and struggles, the people whose constant input shapes our choices and ideas, the people whose philosophies and worldviews bleed into our own. They are our partners, our best friends, our immediate family, our closest co-workers, our roommates, and our bosses, and we are disproportionately impacted by these people.

It is these few people who give us the best reading about what our Set Point is. These are our inner circle, and even though we imagine ourselves to be masters of our own lives, we inevitably become a kind of average of the 15 people we spend the most time with.

EXERCISE: YOUR INNER CIRCLE 15

1. *Make the list:* In your notebook, list the 15 people that you spend the most time with. These are your inner circle 15, the people that, for better or for worse, shape who we are and what we view as normal.

2. *Hard questions:* Now reflect on that list and ask yourself some hard questions.

*   Do the people that you spend time with push you forward or hold you back?

*   What are you subconsciously learning about how the world works from them?

*   What does the list say about you?

3. *Plus 5:* Now, below your inner circle, write out:

    +

    +

    +

    +

    +

    For each + sign, put the name of someone you'd like to spend more time with, someone you'd like to one day be able to have in your inner circle. Write out why you'd like to spend more time with them, followed by a single action you will take to connect with them and build a stronger relationship.

4. *Transform:* This exercise is not about coldheartedly banishing all of your friends, but rather about beginning to notice how you can alter and strengthen your inner circle while actively seeking out new potential members.

    In order to begin doing this, start by choosing five people in your inner circle with whom you could strengthen or transform the relationship. For each, write a sentence about what you'd like to change in the relationship and then a single action you will take to help make that change. This last part is absolutely critical—you only have power over your own actions, not anyone else's, so if you want something in your relationship to change, that change starts with you.

MOBILIZE

Ricken Patel doesn't do speeches anymore. As the executive director of Avaaz (whose name means "voice" in several European, Middle Eastern, and Asian languages), he'd rather focus his time on engaging the organization's 10 million members in campaigns of global interest—to cancel Haiti's debt after the earthquake in 2009, to stop uranium mining in the Grand Canyon, or to promote meaningful dialogue between China and the Dalai Lama. The sheer size of the group's e-mail list, paired with sophisticated organizing and creative stunts, can spark a global conversation and drive change.

As Ricken puts it: "We're about bringing a whole new set of people into civic engagement and the political process. We offer smart, strategic ways for ordinary people to get involved. Our core demographic is a middle-aged mom who gets home from work and has to cook dinner for the kids and has 5 minutes to check e-mail. She heard something on the radio that day and really wants to do something about it and appreciates a service that provides a short, smart, effective action that she can use the small amount of money or time she has to make a difference."

Even though Ricken is working to mobilize a 10 million–strong network, larger than many of us can even dream of, his attention to his network's needs is instructive to people at every stage, on every scale. Each of us can use our own networks, the organizations we belong to, Listservs, and other online communities to make good things happen. With a record button and a YouTube channel, our voices can echo and build movements beyond our circle of real-life friends.

Like Ricken, Billy and Dev both found that the key to pulling off major action was building a motivated network of Rebuilders. Before it was possible to scale their efforts, they both began by mobilizing and leveraging the few friends that they saw on a daily basis.

Our personal networks, although often small at the beginning, can still be the first place to start when we want to advocate for an issue, get a job that makes a difference, or take our ideas to the next level. Eighty percent of job opportunities come from people who know each other. Many start-ups get their first round of funding from friends and family on more favorable terms than they could get from professional investors. In many parts of the world, a whole village will contribute to helping send a child to a university.

In addition to the typical surges of pride and insecurity that come up for many of us when it's time to ask for help, reaching out to the people close to you can feel emotionally onerous. If you ask your aunt for a line of credit to get a business going, and the business goes belly up, you may feel a pang of guilt or embarrassment about it for a long time. But chances are, you couldn't get that line of credit from a bank at all, and chances are, your aunt will be more forgiving and supportive of you than the bank's loan officer.

In Chapter 8, we'll explore the full range of what it takes to make your move and launch something, but the foundation for movement is the personal relationships and networks we all belong to already. In order to best take advantage of those connections, let's break down some basic steps to start building and mobilizing your network regardless of its current size:

* Define your needs. Before asking for help, it's usually a good idea to know what help you need. Sounds obvious, but in dozens of mentoring sessions with young leaders, we rarely get a clear request for help. Your needs will evolve, sometimes even day-to-day, but having a clear set of well-defined needs will help you build a good list of people to talk with—for each need, there may be a handful of people you could reach out to and ask for help. And before each meeting, take a moment to think about what specific talents, assets, time, or ideas that person might be able to contribute so the ask is personalized and in context.

* Have LOTS of one-on-one conversations with people. For some of us, this comes easily. Our fascination with others puts us into conversations wherever we go. For others of us, social anxiety makes this one tough and even a little scary. Think about conversations as opportunities to let folks know what you're doing (or what you'd like to do) and why you're doing it, to ask good questions, and to listen a lot. Be respectful of their time and your own. Calls and meetings do not have to last an hour—they don't even have to last 30 minutes. It's good practice to have a basic agenda for the conversation in advance and to have done at least a little research on the person you're meeting with, so time doesn't have to be wasted on things you could have read on their "About" page of the Web site.

* As you're meeting people, begin to map the field you're working in. Ask each person you talk with if they could recommend (and, even better, introduce you to) two or three other people that could be potential allies or collaborators. You'll start to hear the same names come up over and over. These may be important gatekeepers for certain communities, people you'll want to support you and your efforts (or at least be aware of them). This may also be a sign that you need to expand your circle of conversations and reach out to different communities of interest that might benefit from the work you're doing.

* Maintain an open posture toward collaboration and help. If people in your network don't know what you're doing, they can't help. They can't partner. They can't promote or connect you to their best friend, who happens to be the missing piece to what you're trying to do. The occasional e-mail update to friends/colleagues/family can be an important part of that, especially if your needs/asks don't come too frequently.

* And finally, focus on the people who want to work with you. Often, the people you think you need to work with aren't that interested in working with you, and they will either string you along or just be unresponsive to your continued friendly approaches, which can be misleadingly discouraging. It may be that you need to show some success before they take you seriously and are open to helping or figuring out how to work together. With the Energy Action Coalition, Billy knew he would eventually want to partner with big national groups like the Hip Hop Caucus or Future Farmers of America, but if they had been the first organizations he had reached out to, they might not have taken the proposition of working together very seriously.

DAILY PRACTICE #6: AUTHENTICITY

*"I found that to tell the truth is the hardest thing on
Earth, harder than fighting in a war, harder than taking
part in a revolution. If you try it you will find at times
sweat will break upon you. You will find that, even if you
succeed in discounting the attitudes of others to you and
your life, you will wrestle with yourself most of all, fight
with yourself, for there will surge up in you a strong
desire to alter the facts, to dress up your feelings. You
will find that there are many things you don't want to
admit about yourself and others. And yet there is no
more exciting adventure than trying to be honest in this
way. The power that sweeps over you when you've done
it makes you know that."*

—RICHARD WRIGHT

We all lie, each and every one of us, perhaps even several times every day. Several studies show people lie an average of twice during every 30 minutes of conversation. Most lies are not really even conscious—they are so habitual, we don't even notice the distance between what we're saying and the truth.

We learned to exaggerate, blur, and outright manufacture early in life. Our health and well-being depended on our ability to get others to care for us. Being highly adaptive and intelligent creatures, we learned quickly to play to the approval of others. Perhaps we were brilliant political strategists in our own family, learning it wasn't safe, expedient, or convenient to show certain parts of ourselves. Our families encouraged, even perhaps demanded, forms of hiding.

We then entered our educational system, where we were

publicly rewarded and humiliated depending on our willingness and ability to play the game, socially and academically.
Those of us with social identities other than white, male, and
straight usually experienced extra pressures to hide parts of
ourselves that might deepen our sense of otherness. When we
graduated, we gained passage into a world where the economic,
educational, cultural, political, and religious institutions are
filled with lies.

And here we are. Having denied our truths so often for so
long, having performed different versions of ourselves to satisfy different contextual needs, we don't always know what we
really think and feel. We deceive others routinely, often without
being aware we did so. And we lie to ourselves. We deny the
truth in our own experience—our true desires, beliefs, and
privileges—again and again.

STEP 1: SEE YOURSELF

Lying takes many forms, including lots of different kinds of
omission and avoidance. Do you recognize any of the following
subtle lies in your world or your life?

* Saying "yes" when you don't really mean it

* Making excuses when faced with a situation in which you do
  share some responsibility

* Avoiding mentioning things that might "upset" someone

* Masking your vulnerability with tightness, defensiveness,
  anger, or intellectual arguments

* Not saying "no" directly

* Pretending certainty or expertise when you don't really know; inflating your accomplishments

* Feigning uncertainty when you really do know

* Not letting others know what you truly think, feel, or want

* When disagreeing, failing to acknowledge what you know to be valid in the other's position

* Withdrawing from conflicts that you know need to be worked through

* Not saying directly to someone what you say about them to others ("water cooler" talk)

* Forgetting to do something we said we would do; not following through on agreements

* Exaggerating, withholding, or distorting the facts to win your point

* Not being transparent about your real motivation or agendas

Did we miss anything?

Perhaps some of these lies seem harmless. Many of the lies are self-contained, instances where we're just misleading ourselves. Or there may be some occasions where it actually serves some higher good to not tell the truth. But most of our lies are so habitual that we have a hard time sensing their distance from the truth, let alone assessing their damage, and they serve at best to protect us from vulnerability and sacrifice. And for many of us, the potential power of our leadership is significantly limited to these semiconscious patterns of inauthenticity.

Notice each and every time you do not express the truth of what you think and feel. In each case, examine what you are hiding.

STEP 2: 100 PERCENT AUTHENTICITY

One hundred percent authenticity can be harder than it feels it should be when we say it out loud. We can find endless examples of people who are inauthentic, get ahead, and get away with it. For some, it is these half-truths that actually provide the basis for their career. Seeing and proving ourselves can be overwhelming—how can we compete with people who tell stories on steroids or with images that are so carefully curated that reality becomes nonexistent?

We can find the excitement in truth—to have as our goal not to act as if the world is pretend, but to be truthful ourselves. This is not to say that being authentic at all times means blurting out every terrible or errant thought.

We want to be RUTHLESSLY honest with ourselves, but SKILLFUL in our authentic communications with others. You want to speak vulnerably of your own feelings and real human needs, rather than your judgments of others. You want to address the behaviors of others without needing to expound upon your theories of who people are on the inside or why they do what they do. You want to approach others with respect, rather than arrogance. After all, your truth is only the truth of your experience. They have their truth as well.

To speak our truth even when we feel it is tough, we need

to be relaxed and comfortable in it. If you are anxious or upset when you approach people, they will sense it, and it impacts the conversation. To become relaxed in our truth, begin by thinking and reflecting on your intent. As William Blake wrote, "A truth that's told with bad intent beats all the lies you can invent."

If you already consider yourself fairly "honest," try fine-tuning your sensors for inauthenticity and hold yourself to a zero-tolerance standard. Are there some situations where it's for the best to withhold some of the truth? Yes, but not nearly as many as your anxiety tries to convince you there are. Can you, even for just a few days, be and speak the truth of who you are? Do you tense up a little when we suggest that?

Telling the truth with 100 percent authenticity has real benefits. As we tell the truth, we have less to be preoccupied with, less to conceal, and when we are rewarded, we know it is truly deserved.

Notice each and every time you do not express the truth of what you think and feel. In each case, examine what you are hiding. *Be 100 percent authentic in your interactions with others.*

RESOURCES

* The StartingBloc Institute (Startingbloc.org) runs a training program for college students that provides an amazing 101 course on Social Entrepreneurship and provides an outstanding alumni network for those considering entering the field.

* There are a number of valuable networks and conferences to attend that will give you a good view of people rethinking, rebuilding and redesigning the economy. Here are some of our favorites: Summit Series, Social Venture Network, Net Impact, Business Alliance for Local Living Economies (BALLE), Web of Change, and KaosPilots.

* There is a growing movement of collaborative working spaces that attract a range of socially-aware businesses and creatives. The largest network is the HUB Network (www.the-hub.net), which is connected to spaces in 30 cities on five continents all sharing similar values. Alternatively, spaces like the Centre for Social Innovation in Toronto provide great resources for people trying to replicate the model.

* There are also a number of Web sites, online communities, and content-focused sites that provide a wide survey of the rebuilding being done. These include: Good.is, Causecast.org, TakingITGlobal.org, and Myoo.com.

* Books we love:
  * *The 5 Love Languages* by Gary Chapman
  * *Secrets of Young & Successful* by Jennifer Kushell with Scott Kaufman

CHAPTER 7

DESIGN

"It is not enough to be busy. So are the ants. The question is: What are we busy about?"

—HENRY DAVID THOREAU

Every time we share a new idea, ask for a raise at work, or promote an event, we are engaging in an act of design—whether we know it or not. The distance between the moment you realize that your office could be stocking fair trade coffee to the moment where you're holding a cup of the good stuff in your hand is bridged by design. We can cross that distance a hundred different ways—elegantly, extemporaneously, or tangled up in challenges. We want more from ourselves, from our workplaces, and for the world, and translating these visions into a plan, a physical object, a pitch, an idea, or a product requires us to become designers. Developing a more conscious understanding of effective design is the first step toward ensuring we work smarter, not busier. To put it simply, good design requires us to slow down so that we can speed up.

Often we're tempted to just wing it, trusting in our own ability to improvise and shapeshift, but good design can reward us tremendously on the back end, both personally and globally.

Well-laid plans enable us to have more time, get more done, keep working through gaps in energy and inspiration, and find greater satisfaction in the results of our efforts. Good design is also better for the world around us—sensitive to existing needs and resources, synthesizing tools and principles from across the spectrum of disciplines, and patterned after the beautifully sustainable mold nature provides us with.

The way that Rebuilders approached design was an important part of their ability to make, create, and build in today's environment. Eden Full began playing with solar panels when she was in the fifth grade, experimenting with how the brightness of the sun, symbolized by a light bulb, affected the speed of a small model solar car. It wasn't until her junior year of high school that she realized that the solar technology she had been playing with out of interest could actually impact the world.

Solar technologies were in use all around the world but were still relatively inefficient. Eden's design process began as many these days do, with a Google search. She scoured results for "optimization of solar panels" and discovered that the most common tracking system involved a $600 motor and an advanced algorithm to follow the sun over the course of the day. "I just thought: *What if I could adjust the solar panel just by using what happens every day?* The sun rises and sets. After some more Googling, some reading of papers, I noticed that thermostats adjust to temperatures—why hasn't someone thought about that?"

She created the Sun Saluter, an invention that makes solar panels 40 percent more efficient, doesn't require any energy, and costs $10 to $20. She wanted to take the technology to rural villages, where it could have the most impact, and see if it actually worked, asking the questions about needs and context before she actually implemented anything.

"I had all these preconceived notions of what it would be like to build. When I got there, I realized none of that would work. One thing I didn't plan for was the number of children in the village. I just couldn't have a solar panel lying on the ground when there are so many children that would play with it and mess it up. I realized I had to mount it on a pole, which changed the whole design."

Across the interviews we did with innovators like Eden, four consistent principles of smart design emerged that guided much of the strategy and forethought that they put in before launching. These were four principles that enabled people to make good. Smart design is:

* Contextual

* Interdisciplinary

* Sustainable

* Dynamic

These principles aren't just for big ideas or life-changing inventions. We are often accustomed to making plans only for the big decisions in our lives, but small steps that make up the majority of our daily lives can also benefit from good design. What are you planning for? What next decision or next move could you apply these principles to? Smart design can transform our lives, our communities, and each time we sit down to go to work.

CONTEXTUAL: WHAT'S REALLY, REALLY NEEDED?

Paul Polak was the director of research at the Fort Logan Mental Health Center in Denver, working with homeless veterans and other patients. After years of work and many failed attempts to develop better treatments, he set about to answer a deceptively simple question: Why are these patients coming in seeking help?

He interviewed the patients, the patients' employers and family members, and the psychiatrists, asking them to rank the reasons they came in from most to least important. He then measured the degree to which the answers matched up. The correlation between the psychiatrists' answers and the patients' answers was essentially random. The psychiatrists had been trained to see the problem as mental illness, and worked in an institution designed to cure mental illness, so when patients came in for help, it was only natural that their diagnoses were virtually always for mental illness.

But more often than not, the patients themselves blamed the problems they were having on their home life—issues with family, coping with the loss of a loved one, difficulty making ends meet. Paul came to believe that addressing the patients' poverty was more important to their adjustment than any psychiatric therapy he could think of. He took over as director of Southwest Mental Health, a community mental health center with a more holistic approach, and he started developing job opportunities, improved housing, and ways to improve self-esteem for poor people.

A few years later, he left that job to explore how poverty affected people's mental state in places much poorer than Denver and to see what could be done about it. His wife had friends doing volunteer work in Bangladesh, so he contacted them and made arrangements to visit.

A relative newcomer to development work, he started by spending months just talking with struggling farmers, asking them questions, and learning about what they needed. The first innovation began during those patient conversations. The farmers complained about the time and physical strain of hand-watering their fields and were eager to figure out a better system. Paul had seen something called a treadle pump, a foot-powered suction pump for irrigation, that had been developed by a Norwegian volunteer who worked for the RDRS, a Lutheran development agency. Without the costly fuel that motorized pumps used, the treadle pump enables farmers to water their fields much more effectively and to substantially increase their standard of living. Paul formed International Development Enterprises (IDE) to disseminate the pumps.

IDE designed 10 or 15 different models of treadle pumps, but according to Paul, the real innovation came from seeing the farmers as customers, not as charity recipients. RDRS had sold about 5,000 pumps in Bangladesh when it started, but IDE used rural mass marketing techniques and built private-sector partnerships to sell 1.5 million pumps and increase the annual income of small farmers by $130 million.

In his book *Out of Poverty*, Paul lays out a 12-step process for practical problem solving, but in our conversation, he emphasized that the first three steps are the most important. They are also the most obvious, most simple, and least frequently followed.

1. Go to where the action is.

2. Talk to the people who have the problem and listen to what they have to say.

3. Learn everything there is to know about the problem's specific context.

Having interviewed over 3,000 small farmers in Zambia, Mexico, Bangladesh, India, and many other countries, we wondered how he was able to really listen to them when he doesn't speak the language. "The words are only 10 percent of what's communicated. I say listen with your soul and listen with your eyes. I look for what people carry in their hands or on their back. What kind of clothes do they wear, what are their roofs made out of, what do they use on a daily basis? I always go to the markets and measure the amount of shelf space that's devoted to the different items."

According to Paul, the biggest problem with design and the biggest opportunity for entrepreneurship are one and the same. Current design is focused on the richest 10 percent and thus fails to address the problems and needs of 90 percent of the world's customers. For these customers, affordability rules the design process. But when an affordable and high-quality product is married to innovations in marketing and distribution, it can revolutionize enormous new markets and provide critical goods and services to millions of people. As standards of living rise all around the world, the companies that serve these growing markets will also grow, hiring millions of workers to help manufacture, distribute, maintain, and recycle their wares.

Billy only learned the importance of designing to need after he'd plunged himself into the world of student environmental organizations headfirst, plan-free. It was a year before all the conference calls, one-on-one conversations, joint campaigning, and in-person strategic meetings generated two clear needs: 1) Student environmental groups felt isolated and wanted to work with other campuses, and 2) All of the existing student networks needed funding to hire more staff. Acting on these critical insights is what catapulted the Energy Action Coalition to an 80-plus full-time staff across the US and Canada.

We created the Campus Climate Challenge campaign to bring the youth climate movement a unified brand, lots of new resources, and a platform where groups could see each other and share victories and best practices to. Just as important, we developed a consensus-based fundraising and budgeting process that we used to raise over $10 million from about two dozen foundations for our collective work over 3 years. The huge (relatively speaking) influx of money into the space enabled passionate young staff to work with and train the hundreds of groups that signed up to run the campaign, help build state networks, engage media, and leverage all the victories the students were winning to impact local and state policies. Just a few years later, our top leadership was in the west wing pressing the president of the US on his lack of leadership on energy and climate issues, representing a crowd of 10,000 youth leaders that had descended on Washington, DC, for Power Shift, our biannual national conference.

Smart design is about clearly identifying an unmet need. It is rooted in patient listening and a concentrated effort to understand the deficiencies of current models. But sometimes, you can't understand that need until you're in the thick of it. The act of listening isn't always a precondition of acting. Too many people spend all their time preparing, thinking about what they'd like to do, that they never actually do anything. Sometimes you have to just try something out and change your approach based on what you learn.

Through diving into the crowded field of student environmental organizing, Billy learned that what was really needed was a coalition to bring groups together around shared campaigns that would enable us to raise more resources together. Synergies like we found with the Energy Action Coalition are available in many fields, and skilled organizational weavers are making a good life for themselves and increasing efficiency and effectiveness through collaborations from the local to international level. Since many of us will inevitably want to work on some of the world's most pressing problems—climate change, poverty, disease, etc.—the need to navigate crowded fields and figure out what's missing is especially critical. There are millions of underperforming (and just plain ineffective) organizations and companies that need to either step up their game or close up shop. Forming a coalition is usually not the right answer. So what to do?

One of our friends is a transportation planner who has helped communities across Canada redesign how people get from place to place, exploring everything from bike paths to new roads and public transit systems. She said many of the communities just want to copy some trendy solution they've seen in another town—let's widen the roads and put in more parking spaces!—when research shows that to get more people shopping downtown, they probably just need to widen the sidewalks. They are often left with unsustainable, expensive, and counterproductive solutions because they didn't clearly ask themselves the basic question: What is the problem we are trying to address?

Designing in context doesn't only mean asking the question; it means starting there and having lots of one-on-one conversations to truly understand what your solution is going to address. Whether the problem is eating fewer chocolate bars or figuring out how to sustainably manage transportation demand in a growing suburb—the process is mostly the same.

What do they need, and where is the opportunity? Your ability to illuminate a need implies your vision, power of observation, and knowledge of the space, all of which not only make you more likely to succeed, but also make people more likely to want to work with you.

INTERDISCIPLINARY: INNOVATION IS AT THE INTERSECTIONS

Sometimes a stubborn problem's solution only illuminates in the vision of a pair of fresh eyes. It can be hard for people who have worked in a field for years to break out of the pattern of thinking that most of their colleagues operate with. Newcomers are often able to innovate by adapting knowledge from a totally different field to the problem at hand.

InnoCentive, the "open source innovation company" we discussed in Chapter 3, has learned and harnessed this power of cross-discipline innovation. Dwayne Spradlin, the CEO, told us, "Usually it's the case that problems are solved outside of the discipline. We find this over and over and over again." More often than not, the people who solve the "challenges" posted to the 250,000-plus solvers list have little direct experience in the field. It was an engineer working in the concrete industry, for example, who saw how a tool commonly used to mix cement could be used to break up frozen patches of oil in oil spill clean-ups in cold climates.

In 2006, a team of researchers from Harvard and Copenhagen Business Schools did an analysis of the challenges that had been solved on the platform and not only confirmed this, but found also that "the further the focal problem was from the solvers' field of expertise, the more likely they were to solve it." Dwayne explained it this way:

> "Even though we know diverse perspectives are valuable, we usually still look for answers from experts within the field. Here, what we find is that if the problem could have been solved by the experts in the field, it already has been. But when the problems aren't getting solved, we either think it can't be solved or we keep plowing more money into it. But what you need to do is put it out there to a broader network with a more diverse range of experience and perspectives."

Today there are whole new fields that are opening up at the intersections, and there are thousands of opportunities to create, build, and become employed as a result of new combinations. These fields also bring the promise of solutions to some of humanity's most pressing problems. Since the problems are themselves caused by many interrelating factors, it makes sense that solutions would incorporate learnings from multiple fields.

How might bioinformatics (which uses computer science to process and analyze vast new human health data sets) be used to develop cures for intractable diseases? What breakthroughs will neuroeconomics (which merges cognitive science and economic theory) bring to help us better understand human behavior and design more effective strategies to improve recycling rates or other pro-environment activities? And what are the transformative possibilities in art therapy programs for veterans, as have been newly created at NYU, Colorado University, and cities across the United States, not only for the purposes of healing and reconnection, but also to deepen our understanding of the experience of contemporary warfare?

When she was 16, Sarah Prodor made the decision to become a paramedic. So when she went off to college, she enrolled in a nursing degree program, baited along by the thrilling prospect of attending to medical emergencies and saving lives.

The experience of getting the degree didn't exactly live up to the action movie she imagined, but she stuck with it and graduated. After applying to 40 open positions in nursing, she finally landed a job at the Neonatal Intensive Care Unit in Edmonton. Days were long and the emotional stress was high, as doctors and nurses treated some of the sickest babies in western Canada. Sarah told Dev about the toll it took on her life: "I was getting severe headaches and needed orthotics from standing on the concrete floors for 12 hours a day. I saw all the nurses in the hospital getting permanent disabilities, and it was clear our working conditions were part of the problem. Poorly designed hospitals were injuring nurses and doctors. After a year on the job, I was offered a full-time position, and I turned it down. I needed to get away."

When she got back home from a few months off, she

decided to go back into nursing while she figured out an answer to why hospitals were injuring the people that worked there. In the evenings, she signed up for a course in disability management, figuring that she would get to address the disability-inducing design she encountered at the hospital. The professor pushed back at every unorthodox improvement Sarah suggested, and Sarah felt limited by the course's emphasis on the dry legal process of employment disability claims.

She simultaneously attempted to approach the problem from an interior design perspective, signing up for an interior decorating class at the extended education department of the local university. Instead of working on the issues she wanted, though, she found herself learning about color theory and driving around to pick up carpet samples.

Nevertheless, one of the assignments in the interior design course yielded something different. Sarah was asked to interview someone she wanted to emulate. She phoned a variety of design firms and told people she was a nurse interested in how our environments affect our health, that she was looking to design healthy living spaces. After phoning 10 design firms, she realized all conversations pointed toward the same guy: Ron Wikman, an architect in his early forties specializing in barrier-free and accessible design.

Sarah was nervous to call him, but when she did, Wikman encouraged her. He recognized that what she was really interested in had to do with architectural design. He invited her to start doing research for him and eventually began to take her to sites and client meetings.

"One day," she says, "he just kinda said, 'When are you applying to architecture school?'"

She didn't think she was good enough. "I totally got 51 percent in physics. I didn't have the qualifications." But Wikman ran down a list of different programs and pointed her toward a top school that was more craft based and took candidates with alternative experience. Sarah signed up for a portfolio class at the community college, enlisted a few artistic friends to help her put her application together, sent it to that single school, and got in.

Sarah finished her first work term with one of the largest architecture firms in Canada, learning hands-on what it takes to design a hospital. She was finally in the field where she could make the changes that she had seen needed to happen.

One of her advisors made the special nature of her position clear to her: "You have an amazing opportunity because you have two specialties that don't often come together. You can actually talk to clients from a medical perspective, and you can explain to medical professionals how architecture and innovations are going to help them. You can speak both languages. If you specialized in designing a neonatal intensive care unit, you can become the expert and be immediately within the top 1,000 people in the world doing this kind of important work." Sarah is keeping his advice in mind as she launches herself. She has ended up in a position where her own blend of interests and experiences has put her in this unique niche where opportunities are in demand and the possibilities are endless.

EXERCISE: MIX & MATCH

Simply by virtue of who we are, each of us might be sitting on the answer to an unsolved challenge. With our unique stable of interests, life experiences, and geographies, we find ourselves at the intersection of lots of different subjects, putting us in a singular position to cross-pollinate and create an original solution. The following exercises aim to uncover opportunities that might result from cross-discipline interests.

1. List three professional fields that excite you enough that you could give a speech about them for 15 minutes (usually a noun, e.g., wilderness education, organic farming, economics).

   1)

   2)

   3)

2. List three work-related activities that you love doing (usually starts with a verb, e.g., working with my hands, having one-on-one meetings, presenting to groups).

   1)

   2)

   3)

3. List three cities where you have lived or want to live (usually a place, e.g., Scottsdale, Arizona; Halifax, Nova Scotia; Costa Rica).

1)

2)

3)

4. Now mix and match the nouns, verbs, and places, creating three to five combinations of these items.

Based on the examples given above, some of the permutations could look like this:

I could live in Halifax, Nova Scotia, and find a job working with local organic farmers to figure out the economics of taking their work to market all while having the ability to help out, get my hands dirty, and work during harvest season.

I could be a recruiter for a wilderness education company in Scottsdale, Arizona. My responsibilities could be meeting people one on one, building partnerships with other organizations, and presenting about the power of wilderness experiences at conferences.

I could get a permaculture design certification and meet other people interested in sustainable food systems at the Punta Mona Center for Sustainable Living and Education in El Caribe Sur, Costa Rica.

Consider each string of words and the list as a whole. What are the opportunities that could tie these seemingly random concepts together? Is there a business opportunity? A potential for an exploratory trip? If you had to draw a conclusion from the overall suggestion of this list about what next step is right for you, what would it be? Would you move to a new city? Learn something new? Reconnect with a friend you've lost touch with?

If you had asked Paul Polak to do this exercise 6 months or a year before he decided to take his first trip to Bangladesh, he might have come up with something like "psychology and creating jobs in Bangladesh."

This collision can lead to powerful insights, new ideas, important questions, and maybe even the next step in your career. We each exist at a unique set of intersections—our communities, geographies, talents, assets, and perspectives. Sometimes just studying these things unearths our ability to design something that is creative, refreshing, and new. It doesn't matter how many people have tried and failed to solve the problem—you are the first to be approaching it from your unique intersection.

SUSTAINABLE: NATURAL DESIGN

In 1962, Rachel Carson's *Silent Spring* woke people up to the fact that some of the new miracles of the chemical age were poisoning people and the environment. Three years later, the US Congress passed the Toxic Substances Control Act, which banned some of the most toxic chemicals and gave the EPA authority to regulate future chemical manufacture. But pressure from chemical companies allowed more than 60,000 existing chemicals to be grandfathered in and put the burden on the government to prove a chemical was unsafe before it went into use.[1]

[1] Environmental Working Group. *Nation's pediatricians call on Congress to protect kids from toxic chemicals*. Washington DC: EWG, 2011.

When Dev was 20 and in his second year of college, he applied to be on a committee that was responsible for advising on the review process to the Canadian Environmental Protection Act. It sounded exciting at the time, and after an application and an interview, he was selected. On the committee were representatives from the large oil and chemical companies, a handful of environmental groups, and one "youth"—Dev. It was a firsthand look at the dynamics of two opposing sides fighting over language that seemed meaningless on the surface but ended up having an impact on what chemicals got added to the Canadian version of the Toxic Substances Control Act that Rachel Carson fought for decades earlier.

The importance of the review committee came into focus one day during a conversation with one of the committee members, who explained the practice many companies had adopted—instead of paying for proper disposal of a toxic chemical by-product, companies would just put it in other products, like drain cleaner, as filler. If these laws weren't changed, these chemicals would continue to end up in our homes.

Annie Leonard shot a 20-minute video entitled *The Story of Stuff* that laid out the problem in enlightening detail. She explained, "There are over 100,000 synthetic chemicals in use in commerce today. Only a handful of them have even been tested for health impacts, and none has been tested for synergistic health impacts—when they interact with all the other chemicals we're exposed to every day. So we don't know the full impact on health and the environment of all these toxic chemicals. But we do know one thing: toxics in, toxics out. As long as we keep putting toxics into our industrial production systems, we're going to keep getting toxics in the stuff we bring into our homes, workplaces, and schools, and, duh, our bodies."

Consider all the receipts that pass between your fingers each day. Many cash registers use a thermal imaging paper that contains levels of BPA, which has been linked to cancer and early puberty. Or the many cosmetics, cleaning products, shower curtains, and baby toys that are made with birth defect–causing phthalates. It doesn't have to be this way. Good design can be the answer. John Warner, who helped found the field of green chemistry and has synthesized more chemicals than almost anyone on the planet, has shown us a path to creating alternatives to the unsafe chemicals we use every day.

Chemicals aside, there is a whole range of products that are holding us back and contributing to our poor health purely because of the way they are designed. If you look at the full life cycle of any product, there are five main stages: 1) acquiring the resources or materials used in the product, 2) the actual production process, 3) getting the product from producers to consumers, 4) the consumption or use of the product, and finally 5) the disposal or recycling of the product. Between each of these steps, there's usually also transportation from place to place. We're doing dumb things in every sector of the economy at most (if not all) of these stages. Every stage of this process for every product has the opportunity to be designed with sustainability in mind, and the results generally save money and pay for themselves.

When we look around at all our stuff, it's easy to find overly packaged, toxic, or totally superfluous products everywhere, even if we're not someone who buys an iPod toilet paper holder or a personal infrared sauna from SkyMall. Check out some of these poor designs you may have become so accustomed to, you don't even notice how fantastically they fail:

1. 100-calorie packs—Newly in vogue with people trying to learn portion control, these snacks come individually wrapped inside a larger box, and the amount of waste the packages create relative to the amount of food inside is wild in its disproportion.

2. Disposable water bottles—They not only require 3 liters of water for every liter produced, but over 60 million bottles per day are being poured into our landfills. This is not even to mention that on average, 25 percent of the bottled water sold in industrial countries is just repackaged tap water.

Noticing the waste, ineffectiveness, and toxicity in the world around you puts you in the seat of innovation—you begin to see opportunity to do things differently everywhere. We'd bet if you took a deeper look at your industry or field(s) of interest, you'd find some outdated process somewhere along the line. When there were fewer of us, the wastefulness and inefficiencies in these systems didn't matter as much, or at least the impacts were harder to feel. But now we're seeing islands of floating plastic in the Indian Ocean twice the size of Texas, a toxified Gulf of Mexico from pesticides carried down the Mississippi, oil spills from deep-water drilling, and overflowing landfills all across the world.

In the 1970s, a Swiss architect named Walter Stahel coined a term that has shaped the field of sustainable design ever since: "cradle to cradle." It was popularized by William McDonough and Michael Braungart in a book of the same name and has evolved into a certification system. "Cradle to cradle" means that the whole life cycle of a product is taken into consideration, and all of the materials used in the process of manufacturing are reused, upcycled, downcycled, or taken into consideration during the process of creation. It is what Mother Nature does naturally all the time.

Copying nature actually has a name, and it is called bio-mimicry. Ecological design principles have been a part of indigenous cultures all around the world for millennia. In *Biomimicry,* the essential book on the subject of innovation inspired by nature, Janine Benyus explains:

> "If the age of the Earth were a calendar year and today were a breath before midnight on New Year's Eve, we showed up a scant 15 minutes ago, and all of recorded history has blinked by in the last 60 seconds. Luckily for us, our planet-mates—the fantastic mesh work of plants, animals, and microbes—have been patiently perfecting their wares since March, an incredible 3.8 billion years since the first bacteria.
>
> In that time, life has learned to fly, circumnavigate the globe, live in the depths of the ocean, lasso the sun's energy, and build a self-reflective brain. Collectively, organisms have managed to turn rock and sea into a life-friendly home, with steady temperatures and smoothly percolating cycles. In short, living things have done everything we want to do, without guzzling fossil fuel, polluting the planet, or mortgaging their future. What better models could there be?"

Inventors of all kinds are applying specific design strategies from nature to create self-air-conditioned buildings by copying termite mounds; efficient solar technology by copying the structure of chlorophyll; strong, flexible, and superlight materials by researching spider silk; and resilient and productive agriculture without pesticides by learning from grassland prairies.

From its headquarters in central New Jersey, a company named Carbozyme has created one of the most poetic biomimetic designs. Replicating the structure of human lungs, which have a total surface area the size of a volleyball court, the company has created a membrane that can be attached to smokestacks to capture CO_2. Several other companies are developing promising carbon sequestration technologies using an enzyme found in mollusks to convert CO_2 into limestone.

Nature just seems to have the answers. What other source of technology and inspiration does all of the following close to 100 percent of the time? Janine breaks down nature's design principles in the following way:

Runs on sunlight

Uses only the energy it needs

Fits form to function

Recycles everything

Rewards cooperation

Banks on diversity

Demands local expertise

Curbs excesses from within

Nature has long been an artistic inspiration, from the Paleolithic cave paintings of bulls and horses in the Lascaux Caves to today, but we now also have an opportunity to look past the beauty to the functional designs and underlying principles of natural systems and be inspired once again. The only question is: Where do you want to start?

DYNAMIC: SKETCH SOMETHING

"We cherish our capitols, cathedrals, museums, monuments, and parks, but who will build structures of this stature in the digital world?"

—JONATHAN HARRIS

The cathedrals and monuments of the digital world are growing from the same seed that great feats of design have grown from for years: the sketchbook. Jack Dorsey's first diagram of Twitter has become legendary in the tech world. Simple, clear, and scrawled on a yellow legal notepad, it featured the basic elements of the site that would come to revolutionize communication: a simple box for a status update, the follow and public timeline. The sketch sat for 8 years until Dorsey resurrected it when texting had become mainstream and began to be a dominant form of communication. Sketches around the world are waiting in the margins of notebooks, ready for their star moment.

When we are young, we are natural sketchers. We draw what we see, what we imagine, and the hybrid visions born in the space between. As we transition from Crayolas to pencils and pens, our sketches often diminish into doodles, then to a 3-D box while we sit at our desks waiting on hold. Reclaiming the imaginative freedom of drawing and sketching, even when it isn't a requirement of your daily job, is an important part of the creative design process.

Sketching and drawing are the fastest ways to take direct action with an idea. What you create doesn't have to be perfect. The more you draw and the cruder you allow your diagrams to look, the less your judgment will prohibit you from finding surprises in what you generate. While most schooling today remains focused on auditory styles of learning, many of us are visual or kinesthetic learners, so concepts and ideas only click when we can see them or touch them.

IDEO, one of the world's leading design firms, has a room called "the shop" at its San Francisco headquarters, where staff quickly build models of the things they are helping their clients with. Tim Brown, the CEO, says: "Designers, by making a film, scenario, or prototype, can help people emotionally experience the thing that the strategy seeks to describe. If, say, Motorola unveils a plan to create products that have never existed before, everyone in the organization will have a different idea of what that means. But if Motorola creates a video so people can see those products, or makes prototypes so people can touch them, everyone has the same view."

But you don't need big bucks to draw a sketch, do a wireframe for a Web site page, or make a cardboard or plasticine model of something you're working on. At Solar Mosaic, Billy's product development sessions often involve the whole team sketching out some new feature or page they want to add to the platform, and then coming back together to compare what they have come up with. By getting everyone fully engaged in the core purpose and functionality of that particular aspect of the site, they get great results really quickly.

This kind of design process is important not just for efficiency's sake, it's actually a key to making this process fun, engaging, and dynamic. Many well-intentioned projects designed to help the world fail for a single reason: They aren't beautiful and they aren't fun. Often, progressives are particularly guilty of a kind of thinking that assumes you just need to give people the facts, and they'll change their behavior or come around to your way of thinking. But most people don't act based on rational arguments; rather, they are moved by emotion.

Opportunities bound to make doing good fun, beautiful, compelling, and engaging. A former video game designer named Jane McGonigal has helped spark efforts to make solving the world's problems more fun. She notes, "The average young person today in a country with a strong gamer culture will have spent 10,000 hours playing online games by the age of 21 . . . for children in the United States, 10,080 hours is the exact amount of time you will spend in school from fifth grade to high school graduation if you have perfect attendance. So we have an entire parallel track of education going on where young people are learning as much about what it takes to be a good gamer as they are learning about everything else in school."[2] She asks the provocative question: Can we use games to save the world in real life?

But this is just one of thousands of examples of how creative and interactive design processes can engage and attract a much broader base of support for the grand Rebuilding.

[2] McGonigal, Jane. "Gaming can make a better world." *Ted Talk*. Feb. 2010.

DAILY PRACTICE #7: PURPOSEFUL ACTION

*"I'm also not very analytical. You know, I don't spend a
lot of time thinking about myself, about why I do things."*
—GEORGE W. BUSH, 2003

Although we might not like to admit it, we all want better results with less effort. If only there were a magic bullet that could give us success, stability, and meaning, all while saving us time. We wish we could tell you we'd found a fast fix, but we haven't. What we have found is that by learning to direct our energy with precision and purpose, we can get an enormous increase in return on our effort.

We ran an aphorism by you in the introduction to this chapter: "Slow down to speed up." The failure to invest the time up front to focus our intention is one of the greatest sources of wasted time and energy in the long run.

To help us get control over where our energies go, there are three things to address before each and every significant event, whether its significance derives from centrality to your career, time commitment, or personal importance. The thought of taking so much time to infuse a plan with purpose can be overwhelming, but as you begin to practice this, you will realize the time you save by asking the question makes the few moments it takes worthwhile. As this practice becomes habitual, you will begin to experience the benefits of more action with less motion: You'll undertake less activity and derive more results.

The three things to consider before each significant act of leadership fit into a model Leslie Jaffe, one of Rockwood's trainers, and her partner Randall Alford, nicknamed POP—Purpose, Outcome, Process.

STEP 1: PURPOSE

Often it's the disengaged kid looking to puncture everyone's enthusiasm who pipes up to ask, "What's the point?" But we each need to ask that question. We have to ask the point in big projects, such as why we are doing this work, to the smaller subjects, such as what's important about this phone call?

There's always more to do than can be done, so it's important to determine the true value of a piece of work before deciding where to spend our energy.

Before each and every significant choice, reflect and clarify:

What is the purpose of this action?

Why am I about to spend this energy?

STEP 2: OUTCOME

Once we know why, the next question is "What?" What would success look like for this meeting (or the article that I am about to write or the phone call I have to make)? The more clearly we can define our desired outcomes, the more clearly we can design the most effective process to achieve them.

Before each and every significant action, reflect and clarify:

What are the specific outcomes I plan to achieve?

STEP 3: PROCESS

Only after getting clear on our Purpose and the Outcomes we want do we start to design the Process we will use. Only now are we ready to evaluate the different pathways, actions, methods, and tools most likely to create what we want. Sounds rather obvious, right? But way too often, our "planning" process is: "Fire!

Aim! Ready!" How many times do we launch into activities without any thought as to why or how?

One way to check your process for some of the bigger decisions or conversations is to mentally walk your body through the steps involved. Often in the process phase, our minds can move too quickly. We have a conference in New York. Then the thought comes, "Oh, while I'm there I should really meet with ____." And then, "I really should see ____ as long as I'm in the city." In 60 seconds, your mind has designed a completely insane, unsustainable trip, flown to New York, done all the meetings, and returned home in triumph.

The resulting trip could be a nightmare—running late from appointment to appointment, catching up on e-mails at midnight, and returning home, drained. In planning, take another few minutes and literally imagine your body living out each of the steps in the plan. You will get invaluable information that will create a better process.

Before each and every significant action, reflect and clarify:

What is the best process I can use to create the best possibility of achieving these outcomes and fulfilling the purpose?

RESOURCES

* IDEO's Human-Centered Design Toolkit provides a methodology and process for doing design research from the leading design consultancy IDEO. It has been customized for use by nonprofits and social entrepreneurs and is available free to download from their Web site http://www.ideo.com /work/human-centered-design-toolkit/.

* Biomimicry Professional Pathways, one of many projects that sprung out of Janine Benyus's book, is an online community and educational program to train (and retrain) professionals in the principles of biomimetic design. For the umbrella site to Janine's projects, visit biomimicry.net.

* Not the first (or last) design question you'll ask in the planning process for your launch, but at some point, you will likely need to match the intention of work with some kind of organizational form. Criterion Ventures' Structure Lab is a day-long training session to help people understand and assess the different options, from Co-op to C-Corporation to 527 to L3C to LLC.

* There are a number of organizations that help you find sustainable materials with which to design. Source4Style.com is a Web site dedicated to sustainable sourcing for the textile industry well Cradle to Cradle Products Innovation Institute (c2ccertified.org) has a public database of materials that are sustainable alternatives.

* Books we love:

  * *Biomimicry* by Janine M. Benyus

  * *Making Ideas Happen* by Scott Belsky

CHAPTER 8

LAUNCH

Billy

It was 3:41 a.m. when I clicked send. After nearly 2 years of developing the idea, 6 months with paid staff, and maybe 8 major iterations in the first product we were going to bring to market, we had a customer who would probably pay us if we could get him a proposal in time before their board meeting. It was for the Flagstaff Federated Community Church, a beautiful red rock church just a 4-minute bike ride from the house Wahleah and I had bought near the downtown. We'd met with most of the key church leaders, they were excited about what we had to offer, but we were in such an early stage that we were still figuring out exactly what we wanted to offer ourselves.

I had told Dan, my business partner, the proposal was at best a C+ at 5 p.m. and asked him to do a pass on it. Six hours later, it hadn't improved. We got on a conference call with our other co-founder Arthur. First we fought. They wanted to change the model, and I resisted. Then we pounded out 4 hours of improvements, including some different, but almost equally major, changes to the model, laughed a lot, threw in a verse from the Bible, said a big huzzah, and sent it out. The product was generously a B, but the proposal was an A. Okay, an A-.

My legs shook, and I could barely type—some kind of adrenaline rush, a natural high. We were finally airborne. If they agreed to the proposal, we'd actually have to deliver on all the things it entailed, including a number we didn't really understand and others we hadn't yet realized we would have to do. We had a whole pipeline of projects developing, but this was going to be the first one to close, and we were ready. We had leaped, and it felt amazing.

And a week later, we got our answer: "In regards to the proposal, the Finance Team meeting did not go very well . . . " The e-mail went downhill from there. We didn't have a customer after all. It would be another 4 months before we finally closed our first deal. Four more long months without a salary, with more rejection, and legal and technical barriers to overcome.

The fact is, if you aren't met with rejection, you're probably not going to create any change (or make much money). Developing a strategy for dealing with rejection is just a part of the platform of skills and behaviors we need to develop when it's time to begin a job search or launch a new idea. We also need to be able to find opportunities and funding, locate people in a position to help us, and figure out the best way to set ourselves and our idea apart.

Depending on the nature of your chosen field, your vision, and how you work best, launching is going to require different things from different people. Some of the questions you'll want to consider include:

* How much time do you want to spend working?

* How comfortable are you taking risks?

* Do you want to work in a structured environment?

* Can you imagine seeking investors or contracts, or would you prefer a salary?

* Do you want to support someone's work or start your own?

In this chapter, we do a survey of the four major paths Rebuilders are taking: Entrepreneur, Job Seeker, Intrapreneur, and Freelancer. Our goal is to give you a survey of each, as well as some practical tools that will prepare you for the challenges you'll face as you get ready to step into the unknown and make your move. Of course, we don't all fit cleanly in these categories, and over the course of your nonlinear career, you may bounce through several or do more than one at a time. Making your move is about getting a taste, figuring out which one is right for you right now, and then stepping up and following through on your plans.

Let's shift gears into launch mode.

FIND A JOB

Dev

We often don't get to pick the moment when it's time to get a new job, and so the difficulties and uncertainties associated with finding work can hit us like a flash storm. So it was at the beginning of 2011 for me. I had been spending 50 percent of my time on my own company, DreamNow, and dividing the remainder among part-time freelance contracts, the largest of which was with GOOD/Corps in conjunction with the Pepsi Refresh Project.

Even though I knew my work with GOOD/Corps was going to be coming to an end, I wasn't really prepared for it the day I found out I had 6 weeks left in the contract. By chance, the grants that DreamNow was working on were wrapping up too. I had 6 weeks to figure out where I was going to find my next source of income.

I'd been here before and I knew what to do. I switched into launch mode.

I didn't waste any time. I spent my first day clarifying my personal mission and considering each category in which I could make money.

I knew what my personal mission was—helping people get the information and confidence they need to help usher in the new green economy. I had been working on this already and had a track record showing that I was committed to this mission.

The second step was getting control of my finances to try to extend the runway as much as possible. I paused some major expenditures and got rid of some of those monthly renewable expenses like the gym, and I got out my running shoes. Confronting my finances helped me get clear on just how long I had to figure out my next move.

And then I made my list.

I considered everything—ways I had made money in the past, people I wanted to work with, little ideas I had in mind but hadn't had time to follow through on. Launch mode was about distilling all of the work that I had constantly been doing in the margins of my life and focusing it on the center of the page.

The third day I sent out two proposals to get the momentum going. I drafted a proposal to the people at GOOD/Corps asking them to keep me on for another month, so I could help them do some research that I knew they wanted. I also Facebooked some people who were thinking of hiring me as a speaker. Just getting two things out quickly that could actually lead to money was important because it established momentum, and generating the first e-mail or application is always the hardest.

The next day I went back to my list. I added a few things that might have been totally farfetched but worth keeping in mind. I wanted to write for a newspaper, maybe a column on careers, and I wanted to know how to be paid by a magazine—both things I knew nothing about, but I figured I had enough of a background to pitch myself.

A few days later, I heard back from the GOOD/Corps people—they weren't interested and were scaling back some of their Canadian options. No problem. During this time, I was scouring the Listservs that I'd signed up for through different networks and conferences and searching through e-mails from friends who were sending out job opportunities. One e-mail intrigued me. It sounded like everything I wanted—a progressive social venture looking for a "passionate, hard-working, and organized self-starter who had strong relationships in the non-profit sector."

It was exciting, but it was full time, and given my commitments, I didn't think initially that I had that kind of availability. But I realized it offered exactly the opportunity I was looking for. I could make time. I sent an e-mail to the friend who had posted the listing and asked him to introduce me to the person he knew at the organization. Within a day, I was on the phone chatting with a director at the company and sussing out what the job really entailed. I told him my personal mission and described how this position fit within it—we talked for 25 minutes. After that initial call, he got back in touch. I had landed an interview and started telling him how my personal mission fit with the job.

Two weeks later, at the end of the runway, I accepted the job. As I write this I'm still waiting on a speaking gig, I have ideas for a national column, and some other proposals from the past few days are ready to send. It is all happening—and only a few weeks after switching into launch mode.

Making your move is about doing your best work on multiple fronts, capitalizing on your expertise, your experience, and your contacts to reach out in as many directions as possible. We can spend forever preparing to ask, writing the perfect grant, or tweaking our resume, but at some point, you have to embrace the urgency that comes from switching to launch mode.

Lots of questions arise on the path to find a satisfying job that you believe in. How do you find the opportunity that you want to apply for? How do you set yourself apart from other applicants? How do you present your diversified experiences in a unified, impressive package? How do you get the right introduction? How do you stand out? What are people who are hiring for these good jobs looking for in the ideal candidate?

Here are some strategies we've come up with that will help you find an awesome job you feel good about doing.

DEVELOP A PERSONAL MISSION

When we say "personal mission," many of you are probably imagining that canned, vague line on a resume that can often seem imported from a Microsoft Office template—*Bring passion to an innovative work environment*, or something. What we mean is more personal and genuine than that, a deep sense of purpose that extends across gigs, assignments, internships, and jobs, a unifying answer to the question, So what?

If you have some work mileage behind you, firming up your personal mission may take simply reflecting on your resume. Try nailing down what each entry on your resume was *about* for you, a reason why you cared about the job beyond your personal interests, and then see if you can find a common thread running through your explanations.

If you're just beginning your career, or if you've been in a line of work that hasn't felt relevant to your interests, you can find your mission by focusing on what you're really enthusiastic about, rather than your experience. What set of issues gets your blood pumping? What kinds of stories do you gravitate toward? Think about yourself as a company or organization—what would you want to be working for and doing in the world? Is there a company already doing it, and could there be some part of its purpose you could appropriate for yourself and the string of jobs you will have?

A personal mission is an important part of getting a job not only because it helps you narrow the field of prospective opportunities, but because job interviewers will observe the clarity of your mission and understand that the job will mean more than a paycheck for you, which indicates to them that you're ready to go above and beyond what's required from the position. The clarity of Dev's mission helped him land a position as GOOD/Corps' Canadian representative for the Pepsi Refresh Project. In his interview, he started with his mission, which, at the time, was closely aligned to that of DreamNow's—to help young people start community projects. He laid out what he had been doing in order to achieve the mission, talking about both DreamNow's work and the personal conversations he was having about it. He showed that the sponsorships offered by the Pepsi Refresh Project would enable him to find a new avenue for his mission, while helping Pepsi create and promote its program—he presented a win/win.

Your mission will also communicate a maturity and strength that will make you seem like a "catch," like someone who is choosing them and seeking the *right* opportunity, not just any place that provides a paycheck. Having a strong personal mission will give you a real reason to build relationships beyond just "asking for a job."

Companies and individuals committed to doing good in the world have almost certainly developed missions, and so if they hear that not only are you doing the same, but that your mission aligns with theirs, you will inevitably stand apart from candidates focusing only on the prescribed role. The more you have refined your mission, the stronger your narrative will be for why you are the perfect person for the job.

ADVICE MEETINGS

You don't always need to walk into a meeting looking for money or a job. Exploratory conversations can be a jumping-off point for long-standing relationships and can help you broaden your network, answer a question you have, or help you find the best next step. These meetings can happen at all stages of your career. They aren't just for beginners.

You can use your personal mission to steer the questions you bring to your meeting, asking for advice on which job will help you achieve your mission, or what kind of experience you need to tackle next, explaining what you have tried already.

Advice meetings aren't grade-school fact-finding missions that trend toward informational interviews meant to give you an insider's view of potential careers. They have a narrow and specific purpose and allow you to either seek an answer to a specific question or get to know someone so that you could potentially find a way to partner. Advice meetings are the perfect chance to get an opinion on which of two things would further your career more—attending a conference or doing more field research? Should you launch your big idea now, or spend a year embedding yourself in a company doing similar work in order to learn?

Here are some quick tips on pursuing a good advice meeting that can actually lead to a long-term relationship, new contacts, and potential partners, or a job lead, without wasting their time:

* Make the advice you are seeking really specific.

* Be ready for the question: "So what can I do for you?" Have a better answer ready than "I just wanted to get to know you."

* Make your asks very answerable, remembering the busier the person, the less time-consuming the ask.

* Default to providing less information than more, and give them the opportunity to ask for more information. It will give you a chance to know what they are interested in and will ensure you don't drag on about something that is irrelevant to the advice they have to offer.

* Ask people about themselves and their stories, but make sure you've done your Internet homework so you're not asking them something you can easily find out on your own.

* Ask them at the end of the meeting if there is anyone else they think you should speak to who could help address your questions.

* Keep up with the relationship and follow through on any commitments you make in the meeting.

Bringing genuine, mission-driven questions to these meetings will give people an easy way to remember what you're about, which makes it easier for them to connect you with the right people. You can start right now, whether you have a job or not. Begin by identifying one of the top five dream workplaces, and then find someone working in a department that interests you there. Approach them via e-mail to ask if they'd be willing to pass on some of their wisdom.

CREATE A TEAMMATE LISTSERV

One of the main ways that Dev has found job postings has been through a Listserv that was initially started by a small group of friends. The Listserv was called My Teammates, and over the past few years, it has grown naturally to include a wide array of interesting, active people highly engaged in the "do good" social enterprise sector. This Listserv has become a go-to place for advice, information, and stories, and an endless source of introductions and job postings.

You can easily create your own. As you begin to find your community, choose five friends who represent the world you want to be a part of, and tell them to each pick three friends to add to a Google group where you'll all be sharing events, job listings, proposal opportunities, interesting articles, pieces of advice, and all-around support.

A few pointers for success:

* Keep it informal—the group is for discussion and opportunities. These are more friends than work colleagues, so act accordingly.

* Always be open to having friends introduce new list members— in fact, encourage it by setting a culture of sending introduction e-mails when a new person joins.

* Emphasize the community, not the e-mail list, when bringing on new members.

* Whenever possible, try to get together in person and meet others on the Listserv when you are in their town.

WORK FOR FREE WHEN IT'LL PAY OFF IN THE LONG RUN
Working for free can lead to full-time employment, a meatier resume, and experience addressing a cause you care deeply about, but it can also leave you jobless, in debt, and with some bitter feelings of defeat and worthlessness. The burden of financial reality for many of us means that taking on unpaid work can be a real gamble.

So how do you increase your odds of having unpaid work result in a real, paying job?

Here are three questions that will help you determine when working for free is a good investment.

1. WHO ARE YOU GOING TO MEET?

Will the position give you access to a whole new world of contacts, or will you be spending your days alone or with folks you already know? If the job you are taking involves getting out of the cubicle and working collaboratively, you'll be better off. Whether it's representing the company at a trade show, helping to coordinate an annual charity ball, or attending conferences, the ideal unpaid positions enable you to either get a broad survey of the industry's social landscape or build one or two solid friendships with people already firmly established in your field.

2. WILL YOU BE ABLE TO TEACH YOURSELF WHAT YOU NEED?

Every job involves learning on the go, but as an unpaid intern, you are going to have to know what you want to learn to drive your own education. Interns are often undertrained and overlooked, so plan for independence, take charge of your own training, and leverage the fact that you are working for free to get what you want. If you know that access to the company's internal workings will give you the chance to learn everything you need, then working for free could be a great fit with your self-starter impulses. If you prefer to take direction, showing off your abilities through head-down work, you might be better off somewhere with more structure.

3. WHAT IS YOUR EXIT PLAN?

Hoping that you'll get a job when your volunteer tenure concludes doesn't count as a career plan. Do you want an introduction to a key person at a partner organization, do you want contacts or funding, or are you interested in launching your own venture? If you have an idea, as soon as you begin your unpaid position, you can begin working on getting that introduction or planning your next move. Your exit plan should include ideas and actions that you can proactively start working toward while you still have the resources available to you through your unpaid gig.

BE AN INTRAPRENEUR

"Social Intrapreneur, n.
1. Someone who works inside corporations or organizations to develop and promote practical solutions to social or environmental challenges where progress is currently stalled by market failures.
2. Someone who applies the principles of social entrepreneurship inside an organization.
3. One characterized by an 'insider-outsider' mindset and approach."

—CASE FOUNDATION

Our culture glorifies the entrepreneurs—the mighty individuals who risk everything to take a disruptive idea to scale—but the reality is that we already have many powerful institutions in our society that, armed with the resources, employees, membership, and other assets, are waiting to be transformed and used for making good. We don't need to invent everything from scratch.

Intrapreneurs are the individuals already on the inside who are open to outside ideas, can understand the language, culture, and power dynamics within their organization, and are perfectly suited to propose those changes that can have major impacts.

Our friend Dominic Campbell, the founder of a for-profit consultancy called FutureGov in the UK, understands the power of the intrapreneur as well as anyone. Since high school, he had wanted to work in municipal government, drawn by the prospect of directly impacting peoples' lives. After completing a degree in urban and economic geography and winning a fellowship for graduate study, he got a paid fellowship with the Barnet Town Council in North London, which allowed him to dig into a wide range of work, everything from policy design to organizational transformation. He got to learn what happened on the inside of municipal government, who the creative people were, how the power structures worked, and who actually controlled the levers of power. After 2 years, he felt like he was stagnating, unsure whether the work he was doing was really having any impact. But then he realized that all of the relationships he had built in government and his knowledge of how things worked could be the basis of his next step. He started a consultancy to leverage what he saw as the true power within government—intrapreneurs. He worked with key intrapreneurs to develop a mobile application called Patchwork, which was designed to help government departments communicate and coordinate more effectively. The app was focused in particular on helping government workers navigate complex social service cases, organizing online their contact information and case histories so that multiple government agencies and frontline service providers could access and update them easily.

In order to get it funded and find the initial users to test and implement the system, Dominic relied on an intrapreneurial chief executive he had met at the Lichfield municipal council. The chief helped him get in touch with the right people and pushed his co-workers and staff to adopt the new technology and adapt their culture. He also opened crucial doors for Dominic and the FutureGov team, introducing them to other intrapreneurs who were working across all levels of municipal government. The introductions gave the FutureGov team the credibility and internal support to successfully pitch a tool that could radically change how government works.

"These were people who were just like us, but on the inside of the organizational divide. When insiders and outsiders are able to connect and collaborate, powerful things can happen." It was these internal champions who also later helped Dominic secure several hundred thousand pounds in funding to continue rolling out the pilot with different municipal councils.

In each of our workplaces, we have countless opportunities to bridge the organizational divide between businesses, organizations, schools, places of worship, governments, and individuals. To be an intrapreneur, you don't have to have all the ideas. All you need is the willingness to go outside the organization, find the people thinking critically about your industry or workplace, and open yourself up to the conversation. We all have the potential to radically shift our workplaces.

Here are the four tangible actions you can take to step up your game as an intrapreneur and effect change from the inside.

1. REACH OUT

The first step is to embrace the insider-outsider mentality and reach outside of your company for ideas, thoughts, and context. Start by attending conferences and events, even ones only peripherally related to your field. Ask people for their ideas, present the problems in your workplace, and be open to listening to radical ideas even though you know some of them may be hard to enact within the realities of your workplace. Sometimes, putting yourself out there in public as a receptacle for ideas on how to transform your industry can feel destabilizing, but remember you don't have to take every suggestion. Think of this step as an open-source brainstorm.

2. BE A TRANSLATOR

Most companies and organizations have their own internal vernacular: names for departments, deliverables, processes, and programs. Listening to someone in a different field talk about "harmonized integrated paradigms" or "strategic on-brand activations" clarifies how quirky and singular internal lingo can be. As an intrapreneur, your job is to translate and filter outside ideas into the language of your culture. Pushing for transformations within your company can sometimes be as simple as using past models to build out the business case for adopting a particular purchasing policy. Other times, getting your company on board with a new idea may take partnership, and consultation with other people in your company to develop messaging will help the idea gain traction within the system.

3. MAP YOUR WORLD

Even though you may be familiar with the company or culture you currently work in, engaging in an actual mapping process can really help you understand who to talk to and when, as you build out a game plan to make change within your office. The power structures within offices big and small often differ dramatically, and the power-mapping exercise on the next page can help you get started navigating the specific dynamics within your company.

4. INSTITUTIONALIZE IT

Many intrapreneurs begin their journey tackling a small campaign such as making a shift in their office purchasing policy. But the long-term work goes beyond one campaign or idea and is about transforming the culture and ethos of the company or organization itself. Chip and Dan Heath's book *Switch: How to Change Things When Change Is Hard* is a very good primer on organizational change. Even in large corporations, it is important to focus on the emotions that drive behavior, not just protocols and hierarchy.

EXERCISE: POWER MAP YOUR INSTITUTION

Let's say you want to figure out how to get something new done in your office, organization, school, or some other institution, but you don't have the power to make the change yourself, and whoever has that power may not be willing to make the change without some work. A power map is a basic organizing tool that can be applied for all sorts of change campaigns. It's designed to reveal power, relationship dynamics, and opportunities for leverage to help you become a change agent from within.

STEP 1: SET YOUR GOAL

In a single sentence, at the top of the chart, write out your goal.

STEP 2: FIGURE OUT WHO YOUR TARGET IS

Who has the power to make the change you want to see? Ideally, this is a single person. If a board needs to vote on the proposed change, you want to figure out who the swing vote is or who can bring the rest of the board around to support your proposal. The target isn't always the person at the top. The map won't work unless you first figure out who really makes the decisions.

STEP 3: MAP ALL THE RELEVANT PLAYERS, ROADBLOCKS & ASSETS

Copy the map shown below onto a piece of paper large enough to accommodate the number of players (and roadblocks) in your particular campaign. Put your target, allies, and opponents on the map, according to their relative power and how much you think they support or oppose your proposal. Put their name inside the triangle, square, or circle each person belongs in.

Now add concise descriptions of key roadblocks and assets next to particular people on the map. A roadblock could be

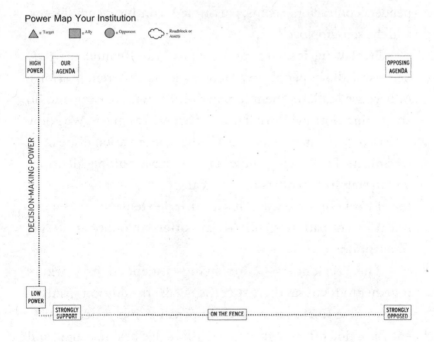

Power Map Your Institution

△ = Target   ▪ = Ally   ● = Opponent   ☁ = Roadblock or Assets

something like "says they can't afford it" next to your target or "has class of seventh-graders who want to help" next to an ally.

STEP 4: OUTLINE YOUR NEXT STEPS

Once the map is done, you probably don't need to post it on your office bulletin board or share it too widely. But you will want to create a plan for moving forward. Review the map and add any concrete next steps to a work plan with specific deadlines. "Talk to Ms. Johnson about how much money is left in the budget by June 10," etc. You get the point.

FREELANCE

Freelancers make up a monumental 30 percent of the workforce. Their ranks include a broad range of consultants, independent contractors, temps, part-timers, contingent employees, and the self-employed.

Freelancing is such a common hustle for Rebuilders partly because it allows people to pursue multiple, different passions, or because it allows them to pay the bills with one gig and do something worthwhile that doesn't bring in as much. We know artist-cooks, writer-substitute teachers, motivational speaker-organizers. Freelancing allows them to have multiple identities and to stabilize incomes in what can be a feast-or-famine sector of work. In some ways, it's a natural extension of the non-linear career path in that it always offers an opportunity for reinvention.

The Freelancers Union brings independent workers together to focus on their specific needs. In addition to advocacy work to fix the tax system that penalizes independent workers, the union offers high-quality, affordable health, dental, and disability insurance. But when we asked Sara Horowitz, founder of the Freelancers Union (and MacArthur Genius award winner), to offer the number one thing that freelancers need to know to help them build their career, she said, "The relationships they have are the most important thing. You can't think about it as frill. Relationships are how you find work, figure out what you charge, learn about ways to sharpen your skills." So the union also has educational and networking events and monthly membership meetings in New York City, where it's based. And it's building other online tools (like the Freelancers Yellow Pages) to help the members connect.

Dev met a true master of the networked freelancing model named Jason at the Hermann + Audrey photography and new media exhibit that Jason was responsible for producing with a friend in downtown Toronto. It was all young and upcoming Toronto artists being shown in a new space, and during the last few days, 3,000 people had come to experience it firsthand.

Jason began his career by amassing a portfolio of small passion projects and clients by attending events, calling up people whom he wanted to work with, and finding small, winnable contracts he could complete at low cost. He built a network of people while sharpening his skills and defining what he had to offer. He finally found his niche a couple years later as a producer who was good at raising money, putting on events, and thinking creatively about communication and programming for organizations and artists.

He got one of his first big breaks when he pitched his services to an organization that had posted for a part-time junior development/fundraising role on a popular charity job listing service in Toronto. Instead of just applying for the job, he pitched the organization an alternative: Hire him as a free-lancer and he would raise more money by bringing the group together with other groups and working on unified fundraising asks and joint events, while also providing a level of experience it would never get with a junior employee.

Jason's hustle worked. He was able to deliver as promised and quickly realized the potential impact he could have as a kind of freelancer organizer. He could work with a whole range of groups he loved, cross-pollinating, changing pace, and never getting bored.

Today, Jason describes himself as a "shadow warrior for notable causes and artists," getting paid through creative con-tracts with organizations and foundations to work behind the scenes to get creatives and change makers the resources they need. He recently founded a creative house called "Ours to Bear," which is now hiring a new generation of freelancers, each with their own portfolios of passion projects. This is just one more way for Jason to continue getting paid to live out his mission to support the causes and artists he believes in.

So how do you start building your career as a freelancer and actually start getting paid for those passion projects that you have going on the side? There are actually quite a few lessons to learn from the paths of the thousands of people like Jason.

BUILD YOUR PORTFOLIO

Portfolios aren't just for artists. We are all building portfolios of our work regardless of what we do—be it a tradesperson or a writer. We already have the tools we need to create one; we've been well trained through the social web to self-define ourselves and become aware of our personal brand, and we have the opportunity to do the same with our work. We are no longer defined by just one title on our doors or LinkedIn profile. Rather, we can stand up and decide how our work is going to be perceived.

Your portfolio often begins with the invention of things you wish existed. Building your portfolio starts with the simple act of creating and completing projects that start as ideas in your head. Whether it is an event idea or a Web site, actually do it and complete it. If you don't have an idea, then put all your energy into helping others turn their visions, ideas, and creativity into actualized objects, Web sites, events, or drawings. If you need money to actualize your or other people's visions—partner with people. The more people you work with and the more people you build relationships with proves that you can complete, create, and stand by something you are proud of.

As you send your work out there, build great things and put them in front of people. You never know for sure what is going to be picked up, blogged, or shared. All you can do is trust that people will work with you and hire you because you follow through. You create and you deliver everything your portfolio stands for.

KNOW YOUR MARKET COLD

Between online search engines and the abundance of industry and trade journals in every field, there's no excuse not to know your market cold. What new tools are improving results? What are professionals charging? Who are the thought leaders? What are the exciting new projects in the field? Where are things going? Good freelancers recognize patterns and anticipate needs of clients before they even know they have them. This can be especially helpful when you're just getting started and don't have much of a portfolio or track record to point to. If you're talking with a potential client, your knowledge and insight into the field can be something you can provide for free, while also demonstrating why you are just the person the company needs.

BE AN ENTREPRENEUR

The epiphany that led to the birth of Emily Doubilet's start-up came long after her initial desire to be an entrepreneur. She graduated from Oberlin College in Ohio with a degree in environmental studies, without the experience she needed to start a business or even a clear idea what that business would be. So she went back to New York City, where she had a home court advantage (and a free place to stay) and attacked the post-college job search with fierceness. Her goal was to land a job with the best environmental business she could find and learn how it all worked.

After lots of interviews and a brief stint at a sustainability consultancy, she saw a posting at sustainablebusiness.com's Green Dream Jobs Board for an assistant to the co-founders at IceStone, a manufacturer of recycled glass countertops based in Red Hook, Brooklyn. She did her homework on the company, and when she went in for the interview, her immediate connection with the company's owners convinced them to give her a chance. Emily sought out opportunities to sit in on executive committee meetings and learned how to incorporate sustainable policies, reporting, waste reduction, and goal setting. Eventually she worked her way up to be sustainability director.

Among Emily's responsibilities was planning IceStone's parties, including a monthly town hall meeting for employees, clients, suppliers, friends, and family. Since the whole brand promise was about reusing materials, Emily wanted to make sure the events themselves lived up to the company's standard. Problem was, it was hard to find truly sustainable products, and what was available was really expensive. The Web sites she was using to source the things she needed sucked. Why couldn't there be a cool Web site that had cheap, stylish products with good information, party planning tips, and all with a movement feel?

Emily became obsessed. Once she began to think about party supplies, she started seeing plastic cups everywhere. Party pictures on Facebook almost invariably featured red plastic Solo cups, and at Earth911, she read that the average American office worker uses 500 disposable cups every year. A Spanish friend actually remembered watching American movies growing up and seeing the kids drink out of those cups, so when she finally moved to New York in her twenties, she saw it as a milestone to attend a party and have a drink from one. Wouldn't it be great, Emily thought, to make a sustainable cup that became just as iconic, but out of material and processes that benefited the environment and the people?

She spent a lot of time on the Internet, making calls to suppliers, building spreadsheets with prices for all the different kinds of products she could find. After 8 months working nights and weekends on the company, Sustainable Party, or sustyparty.com, was born. At launch, it was a really basic site, hipper and prettier than the ones she had complained about, but not much better.

A few months later, Emily spent a weekend at a friend's house and met Jessica Holsey, who was working as an analyst at Credit Suisse in the alternative investments division, which managed over $20 billion of assets in buyout, venture capital, and real estate, as well as direct equity investments in companies. Jessica was intrigued by Emily's idea, and after reviewing hundreds of equity investments and studying business plans, she could recognize a good plan when she saw one. She wasn't yet thinking about leaving her job at Credit Suisse, even though it wasn't exactly working for her.

Emily and Jessica stayed in touch that year, and when they saw each other the next summer, Jessica was looking for a job more aligned to her values, a start-up that she could join and help build, a place where she could be her own boss. They started to tentatively work together. Jessica decided to leave her job at Credit Suisse and invest in Susty Party to become a co-owner, as well as take on the position of full-time president.

Today, Jessica holds down day-to-day operations, handling everything from customer service and inventory and orders to product pricing and financials. Jessica also created the famous Susty Party beer pong kit, found their office space, and throws the parties.

Over the past 2 years, the duo has grown sales exponentially, secured partners including some direct-contract manufacturing relationships, opened warehouses on the East Coast and West Coast, sponsored almost 100 events that needed some extra help to go green, are expanding selection, and are helping new products reach the market one party and one cup at a time.

Entrepreneurs today aren't just starting companies. Being an entrepreneur is about starting something, and smart entrepreneurs should know that form follows function. Today, as we figure out how to translate our goals (the function) into institutional structures (the form), we have lots of options. Sometimes it's a partnership or an LLC, but depending on what we want, it may be that a worker-owned co-op, alliance, citizen utility, or a political campaign is the right match.

But during our interviews with entrepreneurs of all kinds, when pressed for the unique challenges and advantages they faced running an institution built around a concept that "did good," the answer was inevitably the same. "Yes, yes, the business does good for the world, but at the end of the day, it's basics like having a good team, building affordable products or running strong programs, excellent customer service, and managing our cash flow that keeps the doors open so we are even able to see any social impact." The advantage of having a social mission can be a powerful edge, but the question to answer today as an entrepreneur is: How can you do things better, more efficiently, and cheaper *by* building things that are better for the world?

Although we use the word business, the following are general tips for founders of all kinds of institutions who make money and do good as they make their mark and start something.

FIND THE RIGHT PARTNER(S)

Partnerships are almost always better than solo ventures. Having that additional perspective, an additional network of relationships, someone to share the pressure and emotional roller coaster of starting a business with, can all make the difference between success and failure. Often, you need to get the right people on board before you'll really be able to figure out where to go. *Good to Great*, perhaps the most influential management book of the past decade, puts it best: "First Who, Then What."

It's important to make sure that you've worked with someone a while before going into business with them. It's like a marriage—you should date before making it legal. Emily and Jessica knew each other for years, but they also tested out the working relationship over a period of months to get to know each other and figure out if they could stand working together for a long period of time. Once you've split things up and somebody owns a part of your company, it is incredibly painful to divorce yourself from that person. You really have to be sure that it's a good fit.

Knowing your potential partner for a while is helpful, but there are other ways to see if things will stay fun after the honeymoon is over. Seek out an experience—a hiking trip is actually a reasonably good proxy for a business partnership—with ups and downs, long stretches of time together, unforeseen obstacles, and endurance-testing activities. For the depth of knowledge you want to have about a potential partner, this is a pretty good way to get it in a concentrated period of time. Think about their values, attitude, communication ability, and approach to building trust—do they have the skills and way of being that you want for yourself? Do they push and support you?

You're looking for a complementary skill set to your own, but also some core qualities: creativity, integrity, persistence, and passion. Sometimes you just can trust your gut and know right away there's a match. We had a 20-minute phone call and a single day together in New York before deciding to write this book. Sometimes, when you've got a gut feeling about someone, you just have to go with it.

GET HELP

Lots of people become entrepreneurs because they've got a skill they excel at. They arrive at a point in their career where it seems like they should start making their skill into something of their own. Many of these people realize that while they like practicing their skill or talent, they hate (and aren't good at) running a business. A recent study by *Inc.* magazine and the National Business Incubator Association (NBIA) showed that 80 percent of new businesses fail within the first 5 years (52 percent because of management-related problems and 48 percent due to lack of capital). But when a start-up is affiliated with an incubator, 87 percent survive. There is hope.

Incubators are more common now than ever and are increasingly supporting businesses that have a pro-social or pro-environment bent. The Unreasonable Institute brings 25 high-impact entrepreneurs from around the world to Boulder, Colorado, for 6 weeks and provides world-class mentorship, access to seed capital, intensive skill training, a global network of support, and international exposure. Blue Ridge Foundation New York is incubating educational start-ups, Rock Health is tackling health breakthroughs, and Singularity University's 10-week program takes as its mission to "assemble, educate, and inspire leaders who understand and develop exponentially advancing technology to address humanity's Grand Challenges."

EMBRACE BOOTSTRAPPING

When explaining why "Outside money is Plan Z" in the brilliant book *Rework*, Jason Fried and David Heinemeier Hansson list a few pretty compelling reasons like "you give up control," "you wind up building what *investors* want instead of what *customers* want," and "it's usually a bad deal." Actually, any single one of those reasons should give us the kick in the pants to bootstrap it a while, at least until you've got something to show for yourself. A single product or program? We know it's not perfect. That's okay.

So the biggest part of bootstrapping is just keeping costs down. When you're self-financing, it obviously doesn't make sense to pay yourself, but unless you've got lots of cash laying around, you want to try to not pay for much of anything else. This is a stage to practice deep focus, thrifty spending, no frills. Sometimes you need to spend money, and some folks like taking out mortgages to finance an enterprise, but entrepreneurship is fundamentally about managing risk, not embracing it and jumping in headfirst.

The other part is making money. Be scrappy. Consulting can often help you bring in some revenue as you're building your capacity or just figuring things out. Some people throw parties, others sell stuff at concerts and sporting events, some people pick up personal-assistant, temp, or event-specific work—whatever works for you. And even after you start bringing money in from what you thought your core business was, chances are, new ways to earn revenue will come from places you least expect it. Go with it. Nikhil and Alex from BTTR Ventures thought they were in the mushroom-growing business but realized quickly they could also make money through waste management and compost sales as well.

LAUNCH FAST AND ITERATE

In the last chapter, there was a lot of advice on how to design a product that is useful, sustainable, beautiful, and innovative.

It's all good advice. But often, no matter how brilliant the design, it just doesn't work very well in the real world, and you don't really understand what customers want until you see them using some first version of what you've got. So plan, design, and get it out there already, and see what you learn. Then raise money. Then put out 2.0.

RAISING CASH MONEY

If you need to raise outside money, friends, family, and partners are usually the best bet to help get you going in the early stage. This can be done the old-fashioned way through personal checks or through online tools like Kickstarter or Crowdrise. But depending on what you're starting, there are different options for scale funding—government and foundation grants, contracts, membership dues, venture capital, patient capital, and beyond.

A whole new sector called "impact investing," which seeks both social and environmental as well as financial returns, is predicted to be as big as $500 billion in a little over 5 years.[1] The community of impact investors that actually care about both doing good and earning a profit are organizing themselves. Networks like Investors' Circle and Social Venture Network meet regularly and are funding some of the leading businesses in the do-good space.

At some point, you just need to make an ask. In the early days of Energy Action Coalition, Billy went into Mike Brune's office at the Rainforest Action Network in San Francisco. The coalition had almost spent down their first two small grants and he wasn't sure whether the other grant proposals he had

[1] Monitor Institute. *Investing for social & environmental impact*. Rep. Rockefeller Foundation, 2009.

submitted would come through. After beating around the bush awkwardly for a while, Mike caught on and asked, "Okay, so how much do you need?" Billy looked down and sheepishly suggested, "I think five grand would go a long way." Mike laughed and said, "Look me in the eye and ask for ten." People want to know what you're going to use it for and how much you need. It's basically always advisable to be clear about both. And look them in the eye.

EXERCISE: CASH ON THE TABLE

This exercise can be a fun night out and can actually be used to work on many of the previous lessons. It's a way to test partnerships and launch something quickly with limited resources. It can be done in a single evening, with a single friend, and $40.

Find a way to bring joy into other people's lives or figure out how to make your initial investment grow. Or both. Or neither. You can create anything you like.

STEP 1: FIND A FRIEND

It can be one friend, two friends, a new one, or an old one. Whoever it is, all they have to do is commit $40 and have a desire to work with you.

STEP 2: PUT THE MONEY ON THE TABLE

Everyone needs to bring cash. Everyone puts an equal amount on the table. The minimum amount should be $40, and there should be no upper limit.

STEP 3: CREATE A PLAN

There are three rules: (1) Draw up a plan (sketches are a bonus); (2) Create something together; and (3) Record what you do. You can do anything with the money. Notice how your ideas change now that there are resources on the table.

STEP 4: DO IT + RECORD IT

You've got 24 hours or less. Nothing can wait. This is about immediate results, immediate creativity, and working together to accomplish a goal. Record whatever you do, and either share it with your friends or with the world. Pictures are essential and video is even better. We look forward to hearing how it goes.

DAILY PRACTICE #8: COMMITMENT TO YOUR WORD

"The best way to keep one's word is not to give it."

—NAPOLEON BONAPARTE

Our words have great power. They can create and destroy. They can bring our dreams and deepest desires into being. Our words can also wreak chaos, breed distrust, and create animosity. To trust our own word is important—to truly believe that when we say we will do something, it will happen. More than anything else, launching is about follow-through.

When we make a commitment, we create an expectation— in others, in ourselves, and in the universe, and when we keep that commitment, we build power, confidence, and trust. Each time we do not fulfill our commitment, the opposite happens. When we break our word, there are unforeseen impacts for those around us—impacts we will never know. Something unimportant to us can have significant weight for another.

To understand the importance of our word is to understand what it means to commit, to give our word. We learn not to say anything unless we are 100 percent committed to delivering what was promised, at the time we promised it, at the quality and standards to which we agreed. Too often, we make commitments without really thinking through the implications. Or we make commitments without being committed. Being impeccable in keeping our commitments takes some serious attention.

Most of these unclear commitments come from our difficulty in saying no. When we wimp out of saying no directly, we end up with responsibilities we can't or don't want to fulfill, and we typically make other people pay the costs as we fail to deliver.

STEP 1: MAKE A LIST

Make a list of all your outstanding commitments. One list, in one place. For some, this means simply taking your work to-do list and adding your commitments to friends, family, and yourself. Others will need to collect information scattered about in different places—their computer, their cell phone, stacks of paper piling up on their desk. There's absolutely no way you can deliver on all your commitments if you don't even know what they are.

Next to each commitment, write the date or approximate date when you are going to deliver on this commitment. If there is no existing date, create one; otherwise, you'll probably never do it.

STEP 2: MAKE A CHOICE

There are four ways you can react to each item on the list in front of you. They are as follows:

1. Fully align yourself and commit to deliver 100 percent

2. Renegotiate by going back to the person(s) or yourself and consciously recreate the terms of what you agreed to do

3.   "Try" to fulfill the commitment with ambivalence and/or griping

4.   Default on the commitment and just ignore it

Options #1 and #2 build power, help you create better results with less energy, and generally help create a better world for all of us. Option #3 saps our energy and usually delivers poor results. We spend a lot of time and waste a lot of energy operating in this mode. Option #4? You know the impact. We lose faith in ourselves, and we lose the trust of others.

STEP 3: KEEP EVERY COMMITMENT 100 PERCENT IMPECCABLY!

Now that you have consolidated all of the outstanding commitments in your life, it's time to rethink how and when you make new commitments. Step 3 is the heart of the discipline: Make a commitment to be impeccable with your word. Follow through with every commitment that you write down. It's a challenge, and both makes you consider what you're saying when you make a commitment and ensures that you actually do what you promise.

What does "impeccable" mean? It means that you did what you said you would do. It means you did it at the quality that you promised. It means you did it within the time frame that you promised, and it means that it was delivered with positive energy.

STEP 4: REMEMBER TO SAY NO

After a few days of this practice, you may find yourself wanting to say no to more things, but you may not know how to do it. Saying no is hard and can be one of the major obstacles in achieving 100 percent impeccability. One thing that really helps us to say no is to remember what we're saying yes to. Every time that we say no to a commitment, we are saying yes to something else that we've chosen. Perhaps you are saying yes to more time for family and loved ones or a more important goal that you have already committed to. Being grounded in the yes can give you the strength to say no.

STEP 5: MAKE IT A PART OF YOUR ROUTINE

Like the other disciplines featured throughout the book, this is not a one-time exercise. It's meant to be practiced on a daily basis. If it begins as an experiment, our hope is that it changes into a way of living, and with that transformation will come better relationships and a better world. There are several methods that we use to help us make it part of a routine. These include:

* A commitment book: Carry a small notebook that is solely reserved for writing down commitments and their related details. It's (intended to be) empowering to look at and get an idea of how well you are doing as you cross them off.

* A commitment calendar: If you use an online calendar, create one specifically for the commitments you make. You can then easily see when your deadlines are and quickly judge whether or not to take on new commitments.

RESOURCES

* There are hundreds of job search sites that are focused on "doing good" that range from idealist.org to sustainablebusiness.com/jobs. For the latest list that we have, visit makinggood.org.

* Incubators are growing in popularity and are a great way to get an edge when launching. Some of the best ones that have a triple bottom line approach include: The Unreasonable Institute, Blue Engine, Y Combinator. There are also programs that help you launch that aren't as intensive as an incubator such as Fast Trac Consulting or even shorter a Startup Weekend event. A great resource to begin is Startup America Partnership (startupamericapartnership.org), which has a great library of free resources.

* The Freelancers Union (freelancersunion.org) is the go to place for resources, support, and networking events for those just starting out or well established in their freelance career. Members get access to resources, networking events, access to health insurance, and discounts from a wide range of businesses.

* Some of best places to go for startup capital include Angel List, Investor's Circle, Social Venture Network, and the Foundation Center.

* Free by Chris Anderson is an online E-book listing 50 different business models that may give you inspiration. Similarly, The Mesh by Lisa Gansky breaks down the opportunity in network/sharing-oriented businesses with a great set of case studies and a list of 150 businesses across industries.

* Books we love:

  * *Rework* by Jason Fried and David Heinemeier Hansson

  * *Business Model Generation* by Alexander Osterwalder and Yves Pigneur

  * *75 Green Businesses* by Glenn E. Croston

CHAPTER 9

ORGANIZE

So that's it, right? You've reflected on what you want, built your skill set, connected, and designed and launched your career. You're good. Time to enjoy the fruits of your labor. Not quite. No matter how perfect the job you have is, how much funding you've raised, or what kind of transformation you've made within your company, your responsibility is not fulfilled.

Here's the deal. Many of us watch the squabbling politicians and the partisan posturing that have become so common in our politics and just check out entirely. But the shape of our economy and the jobs that are available, as well as the protections for the jobless, are in no small part a result of policy decisions made by local and national governments.

Governments have power. Incredible power. And that power can be used to serve the interests of the few, or it can be used to create the kind of just and sustainable society we all want and need. A brief survey of the powers most governments hold: create money, collect taxes, raise armies, go to war, make and enforce laws, charter banks and corporations, regulate economic activity, establish courts, conduct foreign policy, and provide essential public infrastructure and services like roads, public transit, education, police, fire departments, and post offices.

It's pretty hard to imagine being able to build, much less sustain, a happy and healthy society without the powers above being responsibly managed for the public good. And yet, even a cursory survey of governments around the world clearly reveals they are currently doing no such thing. Political scientists have a great term to describe what has happened to them: They've undergone "regulatory capture." This means they serve special interests, corporations, and the powerful elites and not the people or the public good.

The details vary from country to country, but the story is basically the same everywhere. Powerful people and companies use their influence and wealth to win elections, buy favors, and further favorable policy changes, concentrating their wealth and influence.

Iceland, for example, was a stable and free democracy in the early part of this past decade. It had great healthcare, clean energy, and good education systems, and was consistently ranked in the top countries in terms of lifestyle and employment rates. In 2000, the government decided to engage in what the Oscar-winning documentary *Inside Job* called "the purest experiment in deregulation ever conducted." The government began to facilitate the privatization of industries that had been once tightly regulated. It privatized the three banks and welcomed major manufacturers to take advantage of the plentiful geothermal power. In 5 years, in an economy that had $19 billion in annual GDP, the banks borrowed over $120 billion and began loaning it out freely.

The Financial Regulatory Agency became a training ground for the big banks and a third of the regulators secured much higher salaries at the banks as soon as they showed any sort of proficiency in their work. When the global financial markets began to panic in the fall of 2008 and depositors came to get their money back, the banks defaulted and the whole economy crashed. Unemployment tripled in 6 months, and most people's savings were completely wiped out.

In the United States, even as big oil companies make record profits ($36 billion in the first 3 months of 2011 alone), 45 Republican senators and 3 Democratic senators voted against a widely popular effort to cut just $2 billion of the roughly $20 billion in annual subsidies and tax loopholes oil companies still receive. The explanation is actually very simple: The senators who voted to keep Big Oil's subsidies flowing received, on average, five times as much in campaign contributions from the industry as the senators who voted against the bill.

Think back to Chapter 3 and all the big systems we laid out—IT, energy, education, the arts, health. Each has its own set of lobbyists, its own industry and trade associations that are busy capturing governments all over the world to protect itself from regulation, taxation, and competition. And each has enormous resources and power to do so.

To compete, to give voice, to provide opportunities, and to recapture some of those government bodies, we need to build power from the bottom up, conversation by conversation and community by community, to shape the laws that govern the way we work and live.

Whether you know it or not, by even considering a job that makes good, you are assuming your part in a larger movement. It can be hard to imagine. Movements are so often associated with vocal minority or inspirational leaders, which probably doesn't ostensibly include you. But today it does. To understand how each of us fits and how our simple work can help make a broad transformation become a reality, it helps to look at another radical transformation: the caterpillar's.

Once grown to maturity, a caterpillar will begin to eat everything it can get its feelers on. It eats voraciously, preparing for metamorphosis, its body swelling and lengthening, outgrowing its exoskeleton several times. Finally, sluggish and huge, it attaches to a branch with a thread of silk and encases itself in a chrysalis—trapped and ready to become something new.

It's at this point new cells that biologists call "imaginal cells" begin to appear in the caterpillar's body. These imaginal cells are wholly different from existing cells, so the caterpillar's immune system turns against them, trying to wipe them out. But the imaginal cells continue to appear in greater and greater numbers, recognizing each other, passing information from one to another, and bonding together until there are enough new cells to organize into clusters called imaginal disks.

When enough imaginal disks have appeared (only representing a tiny percentage of the caterpillar's body weight), they exhaust the caterpillar's immune system, and the caterpillar's body breaks down, providing sustenance for the growth of the butterfly. The imaginal cells suddenly realize that they are something altogether different from the caterpillar. They begin to identify as part of a new whole, a strong, multicellular organism. Each new butterfly cell can take on a different job, transforming into eye cells, into antenna cells, into wing cells.

The parallels to the global transformation currently underway are striking. We are a civilization in the midst of a transformation from a grow-at-all-costs unsustainable economy to a new and dramatically different form. The existing power structures are well organized and, like the caterpillar's immune system, resist the alternative structures that are emerging more rapidly every day. Little revisions aren't going to fundamentally change our structure—it's going to take a complete overhaul, these new structures combining into a cohesive whole.

It is beginning to happen. Each one of us pursuing a career that seeks meaning, money, and community is an imaginal cell. The clusters of imaginal cells are emerging ever faster and organizing into ever-stronger groups. The creation of over 95+ graduate programs in social enterprise over the past 10 years and the rapid growth of networks like Net Impact, which now includes over 280 chapters internationally of students committed to doing business that does good, is just one litmus test that shows imaginal cells are beginning to both emerge and congregate.

Paul Hawken's book *Blessed Unrest*, which gave us the metaphor of the butterfly's metamorphosis, traces the roots of this movement to indigenous traditions, environmental protection, and social justice movements. In 2008, Hawken estimated that there were already more than 2 million such groups in 2003, and the number was growing rapidly. But Hawken was only counting nongovernmental organizations (NGOs). When you include triple- bottom-line businesses, companies that are realigning their values, religious congregations, and schools with programs to support justice and sustainability, and the many other informal projects and collaborations underway, these imaginal disks could easily number more than 10 million.

This is a spontaneous, decentralized, leaderless movement—a critical mass of citizens recognizing the same problems in every culture, every community, every part of the world and setting to the work of reimagining and rebuilding our world.

The strength of this movement is found in the diversity of people participating, their ingenuity, and the range of their approaches. One person after another is claiming responsibility for changes in their own lives, aligning their work with their values, and as they link up with like-minded others, a movement is built that is fundamentally changing the course of history.

Successful movements change society in all kinds of ways. They shift cultural norms, reinforce fundamental human values, drive technological advances, and fix unjust and unsustainable economic patterns. But ultimately, they must also reform our political systems through the passage of laws, election of new leaders, or the institution of a whole new form of government.

We know political change can seem daunting. Sometimes it seems downright hopeless. Many of us are rightly focusing our energies on bringing solutions forward in ways that don't require governments to do anything. In the long term, all of that work also helps drive political change. As we rebuild industries, playing inside the system, producing goods and generating wealth through acts that rebuild our world, power shifts. The bigger the local food movement gets, to take one example, the more likely we will have policies that make sustainably and locally grown food both affordable and accessible to all.

But we can't just cede government to protectors of the status quo until conditions ripen for change. Freedom House, a non-profit organization based in Boston, does an annual "Freedom in the World" survey that ranks the world's countries according to the degree of democracy and political freedom, grouping countries into categories labeled "free," "partly free," and "not free." The countries that top the list—Norway, Sweden, Iceland, Denmark, New Zealand, Australia, Switzerland, the Netherlands, and Germany—also top other global rankings for sustainability, employment levels, and even happiness.

This isn't a coincidence. It makes sense that the countries most accountable to their people enact policies that promote job creation, health, and well-being. Again and again, we will find democracy strengthening hand in hand with sustainability, with employment, with laws that reflect the desires of its people. The idea that a government should be of, by, and for the people is one of the most powerful, contagious, and revolutionary ideas in the history of human civilization. It is also one of the most powerful levers for system transformation we have available to us.

Germany, one of the most democratic countries in the world, has become a global leader in enacting policies that have established a firm foundation for transformation—and against formidable odds. While it's one of the last places in the world you'd expect to provide a strong base for clean energy—it's not very sunny or windy, and its dense population makes land for growing biofuels scarce—300,000 Germans wake up every morning and go to jobs in the country's world-leading clean energy industry.

It isn't because Germans love wind or because they've mastered the concepts we've laid out in this book. It's because an assortment of social movement groups came together in the 1970s to form a new political party, the Greens, and organized over several decades to educate the broader population about the benefits of clean energy. By 2000, the Greens held the balance of power as a critical part of the governing coalition in Germany and used that influence to draft and push through an aggressive and popular clean energy law.

The EEG, as it's called there, essentially guarantees an above-market price for 20 years for clean energy producers. It's paid for by a small monthly surcharge on electricity bills. This single policy, also known as a feed-in tariff system or CLEAN contract program, accounts for fully two-thirds of the clean energy jobs in the country and has tripled the amount of clean energy in the country in 10 years. The EEG has been so effective that similar policies have been developed in 63 countries, including a wildly successful program in the province of Ontario, and they are gaining momentum in China, India, and other huge markets.

Around the world, we have similar opportunities to Germany, not just in energy, but in every aspect of our society. The rules of the game clearly need to change, when there is so much work to be done rebuilding whole systems in our society and we have hundreds of millions of people unemployed or underemployed around the world.

Good policies can help us create a world where the most accessible jobs are good jobs helping rebuild our society. This isn't just a dream, and we don't all need to move to Ottawa, Washington, or Beijing to make this happen. We have a role to play in making systemic political change at three levels—the self, the community, and the network.

This is the last and most important step. This is where we

come together to form something altogether new, something more powerful than we could individually imagine.

IMAGINAL SELVES

It can be hard to imagine yourself as part of a movement when you're still not sure who you are, what you're good at, or whether or not your ideals align with an established camp. But notice who is around you, people who would never consider themselves activists or progressives but who are privately arranging their own lives around creating a better future. These are farmers and coders, teachers and intrapreneurs working within Fortune 500 companies. They come in every shape and size, each bringing a unique skill to the transformation that's underway. Recognizing them will help you recognize yourself.

We all have our unique roles to play, but we all must also be organizers, making connections and building relationships. These relationships are a source of strength for each of us imaginal cells individually, but also for the broader transformation.

The human brain consists of 100 billion neurons, each with 10,000 connections to other neurons. Its incredible processing power comes precisely from the density and number of connections it contains. It's the same with this movement. Each new node and each new connection in the network create a new pathway for information to be exchanged, for dialogue to discover solutions, for action to be coordinated. This is social capital, and every single one of us has an important role in building it. The Internet is obviously critical here—we can learn from and be connected to more people like us than ever before. Our Facebook news feeds, Twitter streams, Listservs, and personal e-mail lists are all opportunities to connect with people like ourselves and, in doing so, begin to see ourselves as part of a movement that is ready to drive change.

But even more fundamental to our role as imaginal selves is the simple, old-fashioned conversation. Most of us have lots of conversations each day, and most of those conversations skim happily on the surface of things. We talk of the weather, coordinate who's picking the kids up from school, deliberate about where we want to eat, or complain about some piece of bad news we read online. Nothing gained, nothing lost, life carries on as normal. But every once in a while, a conversation comes along that shakes us out of autopilot, that touches on something that matters deeply to us, and awakens us to possibilities for action.

Remember The Wilderness from Chapter 2? That's the stage of life where we recognize that something is wrong, but don't know what we can do about it. This is actually where most people remain. Too often, we perceive ignorance or apathy when what we're really looking at is paralysis. Maybe they grew up with parents whose expectations for financial success above all else limited their options. Maybe a rigid schooling system never allowed them to explore a creative pursuit that would have used the full range of their abilities. Maybe they just didn't know there was a way to fix the problem they resigned themselves to thinking was chronic.

The great organizers—people like Ella Baker, Cesar Chavez, Marshall Johnson, and Clayton Thomas-Muller—know the power of a single conversation to shift people out of this kind of state. A student once asked Cesar Chavez, the leader of the United Farm Workers, how he organized. He said, "First, I talk to one person. Then I talk to another person." Ed Chambers, the executive director of the Industrial Areas Foundation, one of the leading community organizing groups in the world, calls them "relational meetings" and describes them as the foundation of organizing. Relational meetings are one-on-one meetings, as short as 30 minutes, that focus on building rapport, listening, and tapping into what people care about to help them realize what they are prepared to do. They are about uncovering the deep histories we all contain, experiences that shape who we are.

As we swap stories and visions, we start to discover that we share interests. These conversations build a different base for knowledge, vision, motivation, and power than is produced by media and popular culture. The power we build together is derived from a shift in thinking from self-interest to public interest. This is horizontal, networked power, and it is building fast to match and transform the powers that weaken our communities and economy.

By tapping into the deepest values that we all hold, relational meetings can also give us the energy required to get out of The Wilderness. Recognizing ourselves as imaginal cells can come from the simple act of connecting with others like us. It's up to us to seek out these kinds of conversations, to open up when they come, to be vulnerable, and to invite vulnerability. Whether you find this person volunteering at Meals on Wheels or in the lunch room at the marketing firm where you spend your days, meeting them can open up the path to knowing and meeting more like them. The power of the movement grows with each new connection.

WHOLE COMMUNITIES

At the beginning of his book *Wandering Home*, our friend Bill McKibben describes the feelings he has standing on top of Mount Abraham, overlooking the Champlain Valley of Vermont and the Adirondack Mountains in the western distance, the beautiful region he's called home for 25 years:

> "At the risk of hyperbole and chauvinism, let me state it plainly: in my experience, the world contains no finer blend of soil and rock and water and forest than found in this scene laid out before me . . . And no place where the essential human skills—cooperation, husbandry, restraint—offer more possibility for competent and graceful inhabitation, for working out the answers to the questions that the planet is in this age of ecological pinch and social fray . . . Life, which in most places seems to be spinning apart, was somehow slowly gathering here, deepening, threatening to make sense."

Wandering Home is Bill's account of a long walk he took from the house he and his wife, Sue, built in Ripton, Vermont, (on land that originally belonged to Robert Frost) to the house in the Adirondacks they moved to as young honeymooners in the '80s. The walk catalogs the rich community, the gathering of life, and the spinning back together of a community of farmers, bakers, beekeepers, writers, forest rangers, homebuilders, and carpenters—skilled men and women whose deep love of place is expressed in their restorative work.

Of all Bill's books, which range over tough global issues like climate change, genetic engineering, and overpopulation, this one is probably the most hopeful. Story by story, you begin to get a vivid picture of what a whole community can look like. Each person playing his own small part, but all of it adding up to something beautiful and sustaining to everyone. Bill can live for a year eating (almost) only food grown within 100 miles of his home because there are enough different folks earning their living by providing healthful and delicious nourishment. In a globalized world, the idea that communities provide for themselves strikes many as naive or outdated. Economists will say each community should make only the thing it is best able to, make as much as possible, and use the money they make to buy the other things they need. But this has been a formula for unemployment and ecological disaster virtually everywhere, particularly in poorer countries where farmers who once grew healthful food for themselves now sell their crops into a global market for low prices and can't afford a balanced diet from the markets where they live.

As the price of oil inexorably rises, and with it the cost of shipping all manner of goods around the world, the model seems more and more broken. Why do cafeterias across New England serve apples from South Africa and New Zealand in the fall when their own Jonagolds, Winesaps, Macouns, and dozens of other regional varieties are healthier, tastier, and increasingly available at the same or even lower cost as their tired, long-traveling competitors?

But the logic of extreme specialization also makes no sense from a stability perspective. Towns that invest exclusively in a single industry are vulnerable to factors beyond their control—if the single pencil factory that employs everyone shuts down, the town and community get wiped out too. Resiliency comes from diversity, providing and producing a wide variety of products and services, which creates both an interesting, vibrant community and a more durable economy.

After a century of local economies breaking down, the pendulum is swinging back toward whole communities, interesting places that support (and benefit from) the livelihoods of local artisans, farmers, and workers of all kinds. It will take a different mix of things to make each of our own communities whole again. For many cities and suburbs that grew rapidly in the past 50 years—places like Phoenix, Sao Paulo, Lagos, or Abu Dhabi—the key will be density, a filling in of the sprawling empty space with restaurants, gardens, local shops, schools, and other things people use on a regular basis.

In 2004, David Owen, a staff writer for *The New Yorker*, wrote a provocative article titled "NYC IS the Greenest City in America." He wrote:

"Most Americans think of New York City as an ecological nightmare, a wasteland of concrete and garbage and diesel fumes and traffic jams, but in comparison with the rest of America, it's a model of environmental responsibility. The average Manhattanite consumes gasoline at a rate that the country as a whole hasn't matched since the mid-1920s. Eighty-two percent of Manhattan residents travel to work by public transit, by bicycle, or on foot. That's 10 times the rate for Americans in general. If it were granted statehood, it would rank 51st in per-capita energy use."

New Yorkers aren't necessarily much more environmentally concerned than other people, they just live in a place where virtually everything they need is easy to access without a car. They also tend to live in smaller apartments than most Americans, so they use less electricity, conserve heat (what escapes up just heats your neighbors upstairs), and don't have the space to buy more and more consumer goods that lay idle in garages and basements.

Some of us believe that the greenest way to live would be to buy a plot of land and live out in the countryside like modern-day eco-homesteaders. But that's completely backward. With a population set to pass 7 billion, we actually can't afford to continue the sprawling suburban patterns of development that were pioneered in the United States. As Owen points out, if every person in Manhattan had the same land and resource footprint as most suburban and rural Americans do, we'd see a tide of asphalt erase farmland and open spaces across the country. From a sustainability perspective, the rapid urbanization of the world's population is a very positive thing.

In other places, the broken-down infrastructure of the caterpillar economy will be the perfect fodder for new, sustainable growth. An old 3.5-acre steel foundry in Providence, Rhode Island, was the perfect location for repurposing. Two friends and artists, Clay Rockefeller and Nick Bauta, came together and founded a small organization that undertook a 2-year process to restore the land from years of industrial use and build something useful for the community. Today the Steel Yard is a self-sustaining arts hub with artist studios, architectural offices, youth programs, and ironworking sessions. The place is buzzing with activity virtually every day of the year and fostering collaborations and friendships among the diverse companies and organizations that work there. Community by community, a new form of the emergent economy becomes clear with each local project.

Seeing how other cities in Brazil faced traffic congestion nightmares as automobile use grew, the city of Curitiba followed another path. It created a master plan for the city that included vibrant pedestrian malls in its downtown and an efficient and affordable bus system to handle the increased passenger loads. This single community model has become a blueprint for city planners, advocates, and transit agencies, inspiring hundreds of similar systems around the world. Successful community models silence naysayers and embolden the rest of us.

Some of us are like Bill; we live in a place in the world where we belong or feel attached. But modern life for many of us is transient, and our nonlinear career path may bring us to literally unfamiliar territory. So how do you build a supportive, rooted community, even if you haven't lived there for 25 years?

Helping rebuild your community, regardless of how long you've been there, comes down to three questions you can ask, share, or explore yourself: What has this place been? Where is it headed? What could it be?

Find folks who have lived in the place a while and ask for the history, who the defining people were and are now. Ask how it has changed over time, what's most valuable to them, and what they'd miss most if they left.

Rebuilding from this place of understanding can begin to help you move from an isolated group of imaginal cells bolstered by a few friends toward a community that is rich and supporting. Whole communities become self-aware as imaginal selves find each other and share, support, and begin working to make their community stronger.

Take the extra 2 minutes to travel to the butcher shop, cheese shop, or independent bookstore instead of the mall. It only takes a few visits and light conversation with the individual proprietors to begin feeling what it means to be part of a community in a totally different way than the anonymous self-check-out machine at the big-box complex.

In many places, the visions for what a place can become are well defined and live within local community-organizing groups. The best ones have well-developed processes to identify local needs and to translate those needs into campaigns for change. They represent the values and interests of the public and are often the most effective institutions at holding corporations and elected officials accountable and making them serve the public good. Some have paid staff, but all of them derive their power from members and active volunteers. Join one, make a contribution, become a dues-paying member, or just sign up for their e-mail list so you can stay informed about what's going on in the place you live.

NETWORKED MOVEMENTS

"I am cognizant of the interrelatedness of all communities and states. I cannot sit idly by in Atlanta and not be concerned about what happens in Birmingham. Injustice anywhere is a threat to justice everywhere. We are caught in an inescapable network of mutuality, tied in a single garment of destiny. Whatever affects one directly, affects all indirectly."

—MARTIN LUTHER KING, JR.
LETTER FROM A BIRMINGHAM JAIL

When most people hear the words "social movement," they probably imagine people in the streets organized to speak out about a specific issue, carrying signs and marching down an alley of police barricades. If they're from the United States, many think of the Civil Rights Movement or the Peace Movement; in Brazil, maybe it's the Movimiento Sin Tierra (Landless Workers Movement); in Kenya, perhaps it's the Mau Mau Uprising, which threw out British rule and led to independence in 1963.

Looking back, we tend to think of these movements as sweeping up a whole nation in a struggle for justice, creating an unstoppable tide of public sentiment that makes change inevitable. And yet, historians of social movements tell us that's rarely how it actually goes down. Successful social movements usually begin with the activation and organization of around 2 to 3 percent of society—disparate imaginal cells, outnumbered, but imprinted with a vision for the future. This small but critical mass of people must frame the changes they seek in terms of widely popular societal values. They must dramatize and capture the attention of the broader public, and then be able to leverage that attention into policy changes through legislative proposals, advocacy, and actions.

Even though most of the American public was uninvolved in the Civil Rights Movement, their attention and approval were critical to getting the votes needed to pass the Civil Rights Act and Voting Rights Act, which would codify essential protections and rights people of color had been denied by law since the Constitutional Convention. Like Gandhi before him, Martin Luther King, Jr., faced angry and vocal elements within a movement that called for militant tactics in the struggle for freedom. After years of oppression, people were restless for change. But he successfully advocated nonviolent resistance as a means of dramatizing the issue and also keeping the movement rooted in broadly held values of respect, and even love, for their oppressors.

Civil rights organizers would call on those participating in marches or sit-ins or other actions to wear their Sunday best and to not retaliate against violence. When the images of these peaceful freedom fighters being beaten by white police officers and bitten by police dogs flashed across the screens of millions of TV watchers across the country, support for the movement's goals began to take root. Change became inevitable.

Today, the front lines of our movement are not just on the streets, they are in our workplaces and our homes. The movement is finding voice as individuals realize that they are not yet finished when they achieve individual success. Banding together with fellow Rebuilders working in banks, on farms, in tech start-ups, and everywhere in between, the movement is transforming the global economy from the bottom up and ensuring that opportunities for good work are the easiest and most accessible for all.

The nonprofit world that has led recent social change movements is emboldening our abilities to have a broad impact. Today, we are experiencing a massive proliferation of issue-based movements. Consider the labor movement, LGBT movement, immigrant rights movement, anti-war movement, campaign finance reform movement, racial justice movement, environmental movement, education reform movement, disability rights movement, consumer rights movement, banking reform movement, and on and on.

Within each of these, there are usually dozens of sub-movements. Take the environmental movement. Billy has carried the flag at various times for the youth climate movement, green jobs movement, green economy movement, clean energy movement, community solar movement, and, in the early days, the animal rights movement. There are also movements for local foods, clean water, creation care, solar, wind, geothermal, biodiesel, hemp, as well as movements *against* pesticides, nuclear power, coal, natural gas fracking, mountaintop removal, SUVs, and more. The differences may seem nominal to outsiders, but in reality, they're profound. Many leaders of the environmental justice movement do not associate their movement with the environmental movement, mostly for historical reasons having to do with race and class, as well as strategic reasons mostly having to do with cap and trade and citizen accountability.

But an interesting thing is happening. More and more, people are connecting the dots and recognizing the interconnectedness of these disparate movements. After disasters like Katrina, folks were forced to ask themselves: Was it a race issue? A poverty issue? A climate change issue? A housing issue? Or was it all of the above and a whole lot more? Across the Gulf Coast region, where nothing else survived the gale-force winds, oak trees remained, their roots interwoven together beneath the soil.

Environmental groups like the Sierra Club are fighting for labor rights, and evangelical Christian groups are fighting for climate change laws. Multi-issue collaborations are emerging. And some organizations are abandoning the whole issue-based framework and working on solutions to problems of broad public concern. Avaaz does not segment its 9 million–person list by issue. It imagines the same people who care about human rights in Burma also care about regulating pesticides that are wiping out bee populations. In fact, it doesn't just imagine it. It has surveyed its members and found that it's true.

And even those of us who don't identify with a unified group are contributing our efforts to the movement just by working toward the right goals. Beyond groups converging, there's a much broader upswell of people like us who know something is deeply wrong and want to build our careers, at least in part, around fixing it. The movement has gone mainstream.

The supermovement won't have a commonly recognized name, much less a common language. Its expressions are more diverse than the 6,500 spoken human languages. They include music, art, ceremonies, and silent prayers.

So how do we know it when we see it?

How do we know if we're part of it?

Even more important, what's the movement for?

At its core, the movement is based on the same fundamental principle that is common and central to every major world religion: Treat others as you would like to be treated yourself. The Golden Rule.

The movement aims at nothing less than the creation of a just and sustainable society. In this world, we'll be able to have good fun, eat delicious food, make music and art, read books, and take time with the people we love to enjoy the majesty of our planet. In this world, we will all have the opportunity to develop our passions and talents to their fullest potential, and through meaningful work, those talents will make the world a better place.

DAILY PRACTICE #9: STRESS NO MORE

"When I hear somebody sigh, 'Life is hard,' I am always tempted to ask, 'Compared to what?'"

—Anonymous

Personal ecology—dealing with balance, overload, and stress—is one of the greatest challenges facing Rebuilders. Our final practice is to help you stick with the path for the long haul. Speaking from experience here, we can become consumed with our work in ways that degrade our relationships and our health. We put more hours in and continue waiting for the unknown results. It is possible to burn out—we don't want that.

Stress is real, but it's not directly proportional to how much we have to do. How important really is the next item on your to-do list? I mean, really? I know it feels important. Perhaps this is just a form of self-importance, of taking ourselves a bit too seriously.

There are some days when we have a million things to do, but we're "in the zone." We're energetic, on our game, things flow, our stride is long, and at the end of the day, we're amazed at how much we accomplished. Then there are the other days. We may not even have as much to do as we did in our "zone days," but right from the start, we're off center and overwhelmed, and our mind races with worries and regrets.

Stress doesn't come at us from the outside world, as over-populated with difficult events and choices and people as it is.

Stress comes from within us. An event happens. We perceive this event and a set of reactions occur.

Maybe we start to freak out. We resist. We contract. Our breath constricts. Our muscles tighten. Our mind starts judging, finding fault, resisting reality. It is the resisting of that reality that actually exhausts us, not the reality itself. Fighting with reality is a losing battle. Much of what we call stress is this resistance, and most of the rest of it is our mind dreaming up nightmares of what hasn't happened yet and what may never come to pass.

Right now, all that's happening is what's happening. Stress is resistance to this moment of reality. It can be thinking about the future from a place of fear. The same event that stresses us out—an upcoming presentation for money, a big job interview or opportunity, a relationship with a friend—could also be experienced as a new and exciting challenge by someone else. We have that choice. We prescribe the meaning, and we don't have to resist.

STEP 1: SEE YOURSELF

Let's look at how we generate stress. It comes as an emotion, a feeling of tension in the body and in our thoughts—fear. Be present to the experience of this stress. Do not resist it. Breathe. Open into the bodily sensations that are a part of stress. Watch. Bring a sense of eager curiosity. What is this? Where is it coming from?

Do not argue with your stressful thoughts. Don't answer the questions your mind is baiting you with. When we are stressed, our flight/fight/freeze responses have been triggered. Even though nothing may be happening except fearful thoughts, our body believes and acts like its very survival is in danger. Is it?

We don't have to think far back to find an example. Think of that moment of stress.

What does your mind do? Does it run out of control, getting more frustrated, presenting even worse outcomes, placing blame, and seeking answers that it knows don't exist?

And our bodies: Palms are starting to sweat a little, heartbeat speeding up, a lifetime of associations being triggered, muscles in the shoulders and neck tensing.

In this busy, complex life that we lead, there are indeed many difficult situations that require our attention. But stress is in no way a necessary or productive state of being from which to operate. In fact, to create more and better results, with less energy, we must learn how to act from a place of clarity and centeredness—the antithesis of stress.

STEP 2: MAKE THE DECISION

Contemplate this powerful reframing: We often think, "I need to fix this situation, then I can let go and relax." What if you took a deep breath first and let go of the unnecessary tension so you can more effectively bring your full power and resources to bear on this situation? Would you be able to fix the situation more effectively?

Each time you become aware that you are experiencing stress, immediately engage in a breathing practice—meditative or physical—to mindfully shift your state of being into being right here, right now. As soon as you are aware of stress, breathe.

Then do any one of the following:

*   Tense and relax your body.

*   Use your leadership mantra (from Daily Practice #2). Say it out loud if alone or write it repeatedly if with others.

*   Listen to music, sing, and try to find rhythm.

*   Meditate or focus on deep breathing.

*   Walk, run, move, and get some fresh air.

You can do anything that moves your energy, increases your flow of oxygen, and gets you out of your head and into your body. Adapt as needed.

One of the tricks here is to catch the stress early. The sooner you catch yourself, the easier it is to release. Carrying stress from one experience into the next experience makes it snowball over the course of your day, and the greater the diameter of that snowball, the harder it is to melt.

When you are feeling less stressed, then (and only then) engage in the following inquiry:

*   What is happening RIGHT NOW?

*   Is there a real problem happening right now, this very moment?

*   Or, am I dealing with mental phenomena: anxiety, negative thought patterns, etc.? (This is likely the case, unless you're in physical danger.)

* What thought in my mind is helping to create this unpleasant experience?

* Ask yourself: Is this thought absolutely true or is it based on conjecture?

* Ask yourself: Are there alternative ways of viewing this situation that would be less stressful, and more useful in meeting my needs and goals?

A simple idea underlies this exercise: Stress is a decision, one that does not serve us. Freeing ourselves from the habits of helplessly surrendering to a chain reaction of negative thoughts allows us to make smarter decisions and do the good work we need to do.

RESOURCES

* The Midwest Academy (midwestacademy.net) is now in it's 4th edition of the classic manual, Organizing for Social Change. Inside these 400 pages are all the organizing basics you could ever need. The Academy also offers five days of comprehensive "Organizing for Social Change" trainings throughout the country.

* YES! (yesworld.org) is an organization that organizes weeklong gatherings for social change leaders. It created a facilitation guide that can be downloaded for free from their founder's Web site (oceanrobbins.com). It provides an amazing list of exercises, games, and workshop plans that can be used to organize groups and facilitate conversations.

* Change.org is the world's largest social action platform, enabling anyone to sign on, create a petition, and mobilize their friends and networks to sign and advocate for change.

* Smartmeme.org is a communications consultancy that works with nonprofit organizations to help them build movements. They have some great resources on the messaging and communications aspects of organizing on their Web site.

* Books we love:
    * *Rules for Radicals* by Saul D. Alinsky
    * *The Transition Handbook* by Rob Hopkins

CONCLUSION

Whether you're just getting started or chugging along your path, you can find an ongoing conversation about the opportunities and challenges facing all of us doing this necessary work at makinggood.org. The 2½ years we spent interviewing, gathering resources, analyzing trends, and developing exercises are just the beginning. We intend the Making Good Web site to be a hub for this movement, an open source platform to share stories and find resources.

As you share stories from your own path, you will meet others doing similar work. You will be consistently reminded that you are not alone. The hundreds of individuals that we interviewed for this book are still only the tiniest fraction of the people out there reimagining the possibilities for our future. We are with you everywhere—on your street, in your town, across the entire planet. As we find each other and connect, we all become stronger, and the menu of opportunities grows and grows. The greatest achievements of our lives will be products of inspired collaboration, work only possible as a result of the dynamic insights and abilities of the many.

And they begin with you. If you ever feel overwhelmed by the magnitude of the task at hand, read through the questions, exercises, and daily practices in this book, and pick one thing. Perhaps, in the course of reading this book, there was an idea that seemed to be written just for you, that offered a tonic for exactly the thing you've struggled with. Maybe it's an exercise you felt too anxious to try yourself, or maybe it's a Daily Practice that struck you as important, but too difficult. Whatever it is, pick one and focus your energy there. The results and clarity you derive from following through with one project should give you energy to take on more.

We need all the energy, enthusiasm, and drive you have got at this critical turning point in history. We face two clear visions for the future on the horizon. One shows us systemic breakdown, desperation, an unmet need wherever we rest our gaze. And another shows us recovery, reinvention, the efforts of thousands who have countless brilliant ideas and who follow through on them.

In one vision, we fall. In another, we rise. These visions are actually simultaneous and already playing out today. The breakdown and recovery happening all around us are part of the evolution of our civilization, and the opportunities of our time lie at the nexus—to take part in transforming the world as it is into the world we know is possible.

ACKNOWLEDGMENTS

First and foremost we want to thank our parents, siblings, and families—your love and support throughout this process has made our work and this book possible. Our agent, Kim Witherspoon, and our editor, Shannon Welch, who took a chance with two first-time authors and lent expertise and direction. Our coach, mediator, and friend Gina Welch who stuck with us and to Robert Gass who allowed us to share the daily practices he developed over several decades and who taught us how to find the confidence and path forward.

Billy wants to thank Wahleah Johns, his wife, for her unflagging encouragement to pursue his dreams. Thanks also to Arthur Coulston, who has been a thought partner and friend his whole career, and to his peer coach, Billy Wimsatt, for listening deeply and always cheering him on. And to indispensible mentors and allies: Van Jones, Bill McKibben, Joel Rogers, Sharon Alpert, Michael Northrop, and Jessy Tolkan.

Dev wants to thank his close friend with whom much of the book was talked through and lived out—Bronwyn Bragg. Thanks also to Mimi Warren whose continued questions forced him to continue learning at each step, and to some of the first people who believed in and continue to support the work Dev has done through DreamNow: Violetta Ilkiw, Marjan Montazemi, Arti Freeman, and Ed Keeble. Thank you.

We are both truly honored by the incredible friends and fellow Rebuilders who stepped up to provide feedback on drafts, conduct interviews, help with research, and spend real time working through the ideas in this book. Dan Schaefer is in a category of his own for his significant help in the early stages of the book. Keleigh Annau, Sonal Bains, Rachel Barge, Christina Billingsley, William Callahan, Brenna Carmody, Mollie Cohen-Rosenthal, Rom Coles, Kelta Coomber, Michael Coren, Lisa Curtis, the DreamNow board of directors, Will Durbin, Jared Duval, Elicia Elliott, Emma Feltes, Leah Fotis, Adria Goodson, Jullien Gordon, Kate Harris, Melody Hartke, Lindsay Henderson, Alison Herr, Laura Howard, Caroline Howe, Courtney Hull, Trina Isakson, Jon Isham, Salina Kanji, Sam Karlin, John Kester, Brandon Knight, Mary-Jo Knight, Viki Lazar, Hannah Lee, Josh Lynch, Juan Martinez, Janos Marton, Jennie Mauer, Courtney McInhenny, Bryan McLaren, Nikola Mery, Salma Moolji, Mara Munro, Kimi Narita, Kevin Ordean, Tom Owens, Laura Perciasepe, Steve Po-Chedley, Bethany Pratt, Sarah Prodor, Brett Ramey, Alexis Ringwald, Holly and John Robertson, Allison Rogers, Kassie Rohrbach, Dan Rosen, Beth Rudick, Natasha Sawh, Justin Schott, Richard Scott, Gui Stampur, Jane Stewart, Jodie Tonita, Jenny Vazquez, Caitlin Wagner, Rolf Warburton, Tess Wheelwright, Katharine Wilkinson, Andrew Woodall, Jane Wu, Nathan Wyeth, Adam Zinzan: Thank you.

Big chunks of the book were written at retreats during which we were graciously hosted by Sheila and Dave in Victoria, Jeff and the Summit Series gang in Miami, Courtney in Mendocino, Swanee and Charles in Colorado, and Mark and Kali in Brown Springs.

A special thanks to the Hunt Alternatives Fund, Laidlaw Foundation, Overbrook Foundation, Surdna Foundation, Trillium Foundation, and Walter and Duncan Gordon Foundation for providing support throughout.

INDEX

Boldface page references indicate illustrations. <u>Underscored</u> references indicate boxed text.